SHADOWLANDS

SHADOWLANDS

SHADOWLANDS

BY

William Nicholson

GARDEN CITY, NEW YORK

Photographs of the 1990 Broadway production by Martha Swope.

Design by Maria Chiarino

Manufactured in the United States of America

SHADOWLANDS was first presented in Plymouth, England at the Theatre Royal on October 5, 1989 and subsequently presented by Brian Eastman and Armada Productions in association with the Theatre Royal, Plymouth, by arrangement with Stoll Moss Theatres Ltd. on October 23, 1989. The cast, directed by Elijah Moshinsky, was as follows:

C.S. LEWIS	Nigel Hawthorne
MAJOR W.H. LEWIS ("Warnie")..............	Geoffrey Toone
CHRISTOPHER RILEY	Philip Anthony
THE REV. HARRY HARRINGTON	Allan Mitchell
ALAN GREGG/DOCTOR	Christopher Brown
JOY DAVIDMAN..........	Jane Lapotaire
DOUGLAS	Ilan Ostrove or James Holland
WAITER IN TEA ROOM/DR. OAKLEY/ PRIEST	Geoffrey Drew
REGISTRAR/NURSE	Sheila Ferris
REGISTRAR'S CLERK	Ray Daniels

Presented by Elliot Martin, James M. Nederlander, Brian Eastman, Terry Allen Kramer and Roger L. Stevens, the play had its New York permiere on November 11, 1990 at the Brooks Atkinson Theatre. The production was designed by Mark Thompson, the lighting by John Michael Deegan. The production stage manager was Elliott Woodruff. The cast, again directed by Mr. Moshinsky, was as follows:

C.S. LEWIS	Nigel Hawthorne
MAJOR W.H. LEWIS ("Warnie")..............	Michael Allinson
CHRISTOPHER RILEY	Paul Sparer

THE REV. HARRY
    HARRINGTON .... Robin Chadwick
ALAN GREGG .... Edmund C. Davys
JOY DAVIDMAN .... Jane Alexander
DOUGLAS .... Lance Robinson
DR. OAKLEY .... Hugh A. Rose
REGISTRAR .... Mary Layne

THE CHARACTERS

C.S. LEWIS — An Oxford don in his fifties; known as 'Jack.'

JOY DAVIDMAN GRESHAM — An American in her late thirties.

WARNIE LEWIS — Lewis's bachelor brother.

CHRISTOPHER RILEY — An Oxford don.

'HARRY' HARRINGTON — An Oxford chaplain.

DOUGLAS — Joy's eight-year-old son.

ALAN GREGG/DOCTOR REGISTRAR/NURSE PRIEST/WAITER/ DR. OAKLEY

The action takes place in Oxford, in the 1950s.

SHADOWLANDS

SHADOWLANDS

ACT
ONE

ACT
ONE

ACT ONE

The stage is divided into two areas, one within the other. The inner area, which takes up most of the stage, is concealed by a translucent screen. LEWIS *enters, holding a newspaper, and standing before the screen, addresses the audience as if they have come to hear one of his popular talks.*

LEWIS: Good evening. The subject of my talk tonight is love, pain and suffering.

Of course, as a comfortably–situated middle–aged bachelor, I must be quite an authority on pain and love, wouldn't you have thought.

Now, by "pain" I don't mean a nagging discomfort in the intestines. For that matter, by "love" I don't mean a nagging discomfort in the intestines, either. The question I will put to you this evening, and one which I will attempt to answer is this: If God loves us, why does He allow us to suffer so much? War. Pestilence. Famine.

(He waves his newspaper at the audience)

This is this morning's paper. Last night, as I'm sure you know, a Number One bus drove into a column of young Royal Marine cadets in Chatham, and killed twenty–three of them. They were ten–year–old boys, marching and singing on their way to a boxing match. The road was unlit. The driver didn't see them. It was a terrible accident. Nobody was to blame. Except . . .

(He points an accusing finger upwards)

Now, where was He? Why didn't He stop it? What possible point can there be to such a tragedy. Isn't God supposed to be good? Isn't God supposed to love us?

Now, that's the nub of the matter: love. I think I'm right in saying that by "love," most of us mean either kindness or being "in love." But surely when we say that "God loves us," we don't mean that God is in love with us . . . do we? Not sitting by the telephone, writing letters: "I love you madly, God, XXX and hugs." At least I don't think so.

Perhaps we mean that he's a kind God. Kindness is the desire to see others happy. Not happy in this way or that, but just happy. Perhaps we mean that he loves us with a more mature benevolence. Not so much a Father in heaven as a grandfather. "I do like to see the young people enjoying themselves." "What does it matter as long as it makes them happy?"

Here I'm going to say something which may come as a bit of a shock. I think that God doesn't necessarily want us to be happy. He wants us to be lovable. Worthy of love. Able to be loved by him. We don't start off being all that lovable, if we're honest. What makes people hard to love? Isn't it what is commonly called selfishness? Selfish people are hard to love because so little love comes out of them.

God creates us free, free to be selfish, but he adds a mechanism that will penetrate our selfishness and wake us up to the presence of others in the world, and that mechanism is called "suffering." To put it in another way, pain is God's megaphone to rouse a deaf world. Why must it be pain? Why can't He wake us more gently, with violins or laughter? Because the dream from which we must be awakened is the dream that all is well.

Now that is the most dangerous illusion of them all. Self–sufficiency is the enemy of salvation. If you are self-sufficient, you have no need of God. If you have no need of God, you do not seek Him. If you do not seek Him, you will not find Him.

God loves us, so He makes us the gift of suffering. Through suffering, we release our hold on the toys of this world, and know that our true good lies in another world.

We're like blocks of stone, out of which the sculptor carves the forms of men. The blows of his chisel, which hurt us so much, are what make us perfect. The suffering in the world is not the failure of God's love for us; it is that love in action.

For believe me, this world that seems to us so substantial, is no more than the shadowlands. Real life has not begun yet.

(As LEWIS *exits, the screen rises to reveal the magnificently-furnished high table of an Oxford college dining hall. This is the traditional all-male world to which* LEWIS *belongs. Round the table sit* CHRISTOPHER RILEY, HARRY HARRINGTON, MAURICE OAKLEY, ALAN GREGG, *and* MAJOR WARNIE LEWIS. *A ripple of laughter rises from the table.* RILEY *is holding forth)*

OAKLEY: Then she said, "Oh yes, I know, The unspeakable in pursuit of the inedible."

(WARNIE *is drinking more than is good for him)*

RILEY: I said to the lady on my left that animals are merciless killers, and regularly eat one another alive. We had a short, and I thought, productive exchange about the moral superiority of herbivores to carnivores, at the end of which I suggested the logic of her position was that she should execute her cats. She then said, "Why are you trying to upset me? You don't even know me."

(LEWIS *enters and takes his place at the table during this speech.* GREGG, *to whom* RILEY's *argument has chiefly been addressed, responds with common-man vigor)*

GREGG: So? What's that supposed to prove?

LEWIS: I think Christopher means us to conclude that women are different.

RILEY: Thank you, Jack. Women are different.

GREGG: It seems to me the poor woman was clearly terrified.

LEWIS: I like her saying, "Why are you upsetting me? You don't even know me." She's right, of course. One does only seek to distress one's friends.

GREGG: Different in what way, exactly?

RILEY: The point is this, Alan. She was unable to distinguish between an intellectual attack and an emotional attack.

HARRINGTON: Even so, Christopher, some women are very clever, you know.

OAKLEY: Jack, you don't hold with this, do you? You're a great respecter of women.

RILEY: Hah! It's all that depth of personal experience.

LEWIS: Christopher believes only practising fornicators can teach him sexual morality. Or do you believe each man must fornicate for himself? I've never been quite clear.

RILEY: In a sense, perhaps I do. Morality presupposes choices. The man who has never fornicated, or wanted to fornicate, or imagined fornicating, has no real moral choice in the matter. To fornicate or not to fornicate, that is the question.

LEWIS: Ah, Christopher. Beware solipsism. Soon you'll be believing if it hasn't happened to you, it doesn't exist.

RILEY: I'm sure you're right, Jack. Already I believe if it hasn't happened to me, it doesn't matter.

HARRINGTON: Come along now, Jack. We're relying on you to speak up for the weaker sex.

RILEY: Yes, Jack, why not? You're a writer of fantasies.

LEWIS: I do talk to women, Christopher.

RILEY: Really?

LEWIS: Really.

RILEY: Name one woman you've spoken to this week.

LEWIS: I addressed a conference of women on Monday, as it happens.

RILEY: Ah, but did they address you?

LEWIS: I get letters. Women write me letters.

RILEY: Do you write back?

LEWIS: Yes, of course.

RILEY: Pen pals. Well, well. Epistolary intimacies. *Liaisons dangereuses.*

LEWIS: I don't profess any special insights on the subjects. Harry here's the married man.

HARRINGTON: Speaking of which . . .

LEWIS: Yes, off you go.

GREGG: I must be off too.

(This leads to a general move to leave the table. HARRINGTON *and* GREGG *exit.* RILEY *is on the point of leaving when* WARNIE, *a little drunk, rises and starts to recite)*

WARNIE: 'Twas an evening in November,
  As I very well remember
  I was walking down the street
    in drunken pride,
  My knees were all a flutter
  So I lay down in the gutter,
  And a pig came up and lay down by my side.
  As I lay there in the gutter
  Thinking thoughts I could not utter,
  A lady passing by was heard to say:
  'You can tell a man who boozes,
  By the company he chooses.'
  And the pig got up and slowly walked away.

  (RILEY *and* LEWIS *exchange a glance)*

RILEY: Goodnight, Lewis Major. Goodnight, Lewis Minor.

LEWIS: Goodnight, Christopher.

(RILEY *exits*)

LEWIS: You and your pig. Come on, big brother.

(He knows WARNIE *is drunk, and he is discreetly protective of him. Both leave the inner set. The screen falls. They put on hats and scarves, and stroll slowly home in front of the screen)*

WARNIE: Thanks for the dinner, Jack.

LEWIS: Decent claret, I thought.

WARNIE: Very decent.

LEWIS: Shall we treat ourselves to a cab?

WARNIE: Oh no. I think I'm up to a toddle.

LEWIS: Whatever you say, Warnie.

(GREGG *passes by on his bicycle, heading home)*

GREGG: Goodnight.

(They wish him goodnight)

WARNIE: That young Gregg. Hasn't quite got it, has he?

LEWIS: He's alright. Give him time.

WARNIE: Young people are so serious. Though no more than us, I dare say. Matter of style.

LEWIS: Christopher used to be quite serious. I remember him getting quite heated about the abdication.

WARNIE: Thought the king was unfairly treated, did he?

LEWIS: No, no. He thought he ought to be guillotined.

WARNIE: Tell you something I've noticed, Jack. Christopher lives the life of a monk, and talks about nothing but women. Harry's married, and never says a word about his wife.

LEWIS: What shall we conclude from that, Warnie? That women are more interesting in theory than in practice?

WARNIE: I find it safer never to conclude anything.

(LEWIS *stands gazing up at the night sky)*

LEWIS: Going to be a frost tonight.

WARNIE: Too many stars. Confuses me.

LEWIS: Oh, Warnie. You're as bad as Christopher.

WARNIE: Good dinner. Always is. Goodnight Jack.

LEWIS: Good night, Warnie.

(WARNIE *exits. The screen rises to reveal the study at the Kilns,* LEWIS*'s home.* LEWIS *enters, and pulls a dressing gown on over his jacket)*

LEWIS: Here he lies where he longed to be,
Home is the sailor, home from sea,
And the hunter home from the hill.

(The set is dominated by a giant wardrobe at the back. It is the size a normal wardrobe would appear to a small child. LEWIS *goes to his desk and settles down to writing letters. For a few moments, there is silence. The lights change, to indicate that it is now morning.* WARNIE *enters, carrying a tray of breakfast, the morning paper and the morning post. In what is clearly a familiar procedure, he pauses as he passes* LEWIS *at his desk, and* LEWIS *reaches up and takes the letters from the tray.* WARNIE *then sets down the tray, and pours them both coffee, while* LEWIS *flicks through the letters. He selects an airmail letter to read first. Their conversation now has the appearance of dialogue, but really it is two intersecting monologues; the fruit of the long years they have lived together)*

WARNIE: I had the strangest dream last night.

LEWIS: Another dispatch from Mrs. Gresham.

WARNIE: Can't remember any of it.

LEWIS: The Jewish Communist Christian American.

WARNIE: You may ask me how I know it was strange, if I've forgotten it. Can't answer that one.

(He settles down with his paper. LEWIS *reads his letter)*

LEWIS: She's very persistent. "Which would you rather be, Mr. Lewis? The child caught in the magic spell, or the magician casting it?"

WARNIE: No news, of course. Never is any.

LEWIS: I find that I'm quite curious about her.

WARNIE: About who?

LEWIS: Mrs. Gresham.

WARNIE: Why's that?

LEWIS: Her letters are unusual. She writes as if she knows me.

WARNIE: How can she?

LEWIS: I don't know. I suppose she's read my books.

WARNIE: I expect it's just the American style. Americans don't understand about inhibitions.

LEWIS: She's called Joy.

WARNIE: One can't hold her responsible for that.

(LEWIS *comes upon a surprising section in the letter. He takes it and shows it to* WARNIE)

LEWIS: Look at that, Warnie. Top line.

WARNIE: She's coming to England.

LEWIS: Yes.

WARNIE: "I'm told you share a house with your brother, Major Lewis." Who can have told her that?

LEWIS: You remember that American who came and wrote a sort of book about me? She knows him.

WARNIE: Ah. "I imagine you telling your brother about me and him saying, 'Is she a nut?' And you weighing this letter in one hand as if to weigh my respectability and saying, 'I'm not sure.' " *(He gives the letter back)* Is she a nut?

(LEWIS *smiles and weighs the letter in his hand*)

LEWIS: I'm not sure.

WARNIE: She seems to want to meet you.

LEWIS: Us.

WARNIE: Politeness.

LEWIS: A good sign.

WARNIE: You are curious.

LEWIS: When you correspond with someone, you do begin to form an impression. You wonder whether the impression is correct. Now, what do you say, Warnie? I see her as rather short and dumpy.

WARNIE: Spectacles.

LEWIS: Certainly not a beauty.

WARNIE: Long, pointed nose.

LEWIS: Leopard–skin coat and red hat. Brown eyes.

WARNIE: Beady.

LEWIS: No, I don't think so. More, probing.

WARNIE: Pushy.

LEWIS: She suggests tea, in a hotel. That shows some delicacy, I think.

WARNIE: Tea is safe. A hotel is safe.

LEWIS: Shall we say yes?

WARNIE: She might be mad. Remember the one who put an announcement in the papers saying you'd married her?

LEWIS: Oh, I don't think so. Though she does write poems.

WARNIE: Then she is bonkers.

LEWIS: It is possible.

WARNIE: I suppose if she's coming all the way from New York to see you . . .

LEWIS: Good heavens, Warnie, what gives you that idea? No, I'm just a day excursion. Blenheim Palace. Wookey Hole. Tea with the Lewis brothers.

WARNIE: With you.

LEWIS: I'm not going alone.

WARNIE: Well. If you want to, Jack.

(They leave the inner set. The screen falls. The downstage area becomes the tea room of an Oxford hotel. WARNIE *and* LEWIS *look around with some uncertainty)*

WARNIE: How will we know which one is her?

LEWIS: I suppose her little boy will be with her.

WARNIE: What if there are two middle–aged ladies with small boys?

LEWIS: We must hope they don't all want to have tea with us.

(A woman enters, crossing the stage)

LEWIS: Now there's a woman. Good afternoon.

WOMAN: Good afternoon.

(She exits)

LEWIS: You see, no little boy.

WARNIE: What's the boy's name?

LEWIS: Douglas.

WARNIE: You won't be too agreeable, will you, Jack?

LEWIS: Don't worry, Warnie. We'll put her back on the 4:57 to Paddington.

WARNIE: She'll turn out to be writing a dissertation on your works. She'll ask if she can come and watch you while you create. She'll say, "I'll sit in a corner and you'll never know I'm there." She'll ask you how you get your ideas. She'll take flash photographs.

LEWIS: It's only tea. An hour or so of polite conversation. Then we go home, and everything goes on just the way it always has.

(An eight-year-old boy enters and looks round. He carries a book. This is DOUGLAS. A sensible-looking woman follows the boy and looks round the

room. She looks neither mad nor obviously American. In fact, she is rather attractive. This is JOY)

LEWIS: It's her, Warnie.

WARNIE: Surely not?

LEWIS: I think so.

(JOY *sees them and crosses the room to them. They rise. She holds out her hand*)

JOY: Mr. Lewis?

LEWIS: Mrs. Gresham?

JOY: I'm Joy Gresham.

LEWIS: How do you do? This is my brother, Major Lewis.

JOY: Major Lewis. And this is Douglas.

(DOUGLAS *is standing staring at* LEWIS)

LEWIS: Hello, Douglas.

DOUGLAS: Is that him?

JOY: That's him.

DOUGLAS: It doesn't look like him.

(This produces a general laugh)

LEWIS: I'm sorry, Douglas. Yours is, I'm afraid, a common reaction. Please sit down, Mrs. Gresham, and we'll summon up some tea. Warnie, would you mind ringing the old whatsis. That is, if you drink tea.

JOY: Of course. This is England.

LEWIS: So it is.

(WARNIE *has rung the bell for the waiter who appears*)

WARNIE: Tea for three, please.

LEWIS: I get the feeling you share Douglas' opinion. I don't look like him.

JOY: Oh, I'm sorry. It's just that I've imagined this moment.

LEWIS: And it's not as you imagined?

JOY: Not exactly. It's kind of you to find time to meet me. So many people must write you. You can't be forever having tea with strange women.

LEWIS: Not completely strange, Mrs. Gresham. I've enjoyed our correspondence.

JOY: Enjoyed? Okay.

LEWIS: Not the word you would use?

JOY: Your letters have been the most important thing in my life.

LEWIS: Oh dear.

JOY: But let's pretend I didn't say that. This is tea. This is England.

(They sit)

LEWIS: So—how long have you been in the country?

JOY: Just over a week.

LEWIS: And what brings you to England?

JOY: Oh, well . . . I've wanted to come for some time.

WARNIE: So how do you find England, Mrs. Gresham?

JOY: Quiet. Extremely quiet. I would go so far as to say, too quiet. The big mystery about the English is, where are they all? And why are they all so tired? Seriously. They don't talk. They don't move. All day they're timid and lethargic. What's going on?

LEWIS: Do you have an explanation?

JOY: I have a theory. My theory goes like this. The English are nocturnal creatures. They do their living at night. Somewhere in England there's this

terrific party going on, all through the night, with
everyone yelling and stomping and having one
hell of a time. So all day, they're sleeping it off.

LEWIS: If only it were true. I'm afraid we don't have
the famous energy of New York.

JOY: You can keep New York.

WARNIE: You're a New Yorker, are you, Mrs.
Gresham?

JOY: Not any more.

WARNIE: What does your husband do?

JOY: Bill? Bill's a writer. Or he would be, if he ever
wrote.

WARNIE: And you too, Jack tells me.

JOY: All in the past. You call him Jack?

LEWIS: From when I was four years old. I never liked
the name Clive.

JOY: I wouldn't have thought of you as a Jack. But
now that you say it, yes, you do look like a Jack.

LEWIS: What does a Jack look like?

JOY: Not at all spiritual.

LEWIS: Now I've disappointed you.

JOY: No. You're just becoming real, that's all.

LEWIS: I'm delighted to hear it.

DOUGLAS: Mom? Will he write in my book?

JOY: We'll have to ask him, won't we? Douglas has brought one of his Narnia books.

LEWIS: One of the Narnia books, have you really? What have you got there? (DOUGLAS *gives* LEWIS *his book) The Magician's Nephew.* Very good.

(He takes out a pen and writes on the flyleaf)

DOUGLAS: It's not true, is it?

LEWIS: That depends what you mean by true. It's a story.

DOUGLAS: Digory put on the magic ring, and it magicked him into a palace, where there was this beautiful queen, except she was really a witch, and he found a magic apple, and he brought it back for his mother, and she was very sick, and she got well again.

LEWIS: That sounds like a fair synopsis.

DOUGLAS: But it isn't true.

LEWIS: It's true in the story. There you are.

DOUGLAS: Can you do magic?

LEWIS: No. I'm afraid not.

DOUGLAS: Mom, can I be excused?

JOY: Is it alright if he runs around?

LEWIS: Runs around? I don't see why not.

JOY: Don't go too far, darling. *(DOUGLAS exits)* All this "It isn't true" is his way of saying "I want it to be true." I was just like that at his age. I remember actually announcing to my parents that I had become an atheist.

LEWIS: You mean you secretly wanted to believe in God?

JOY: In something, at least. But I didn't know that then.

LEWIS: If I remember correctly, you've been through several phases. You were born a Jew, then you came a Communist and then you converted to Christianity.

JOY: You remember correctly.

LEWIS: But you started with atheism?

JOY: No, I started with materialism. I had it all worked out by high school. Men are only apes.

LEWIS: Thanks very much.

JOY: Life is only an electrochemical reaction. Mind is only a set of conditioned reflexes. And, anyway, most people aren't rational like me. The universe is only matter. Matter is only energy. I forget what I said energy was only.

WARNIE: Extraordinary.

JOY: Oh, that was all a front. Somewhere deep inside there was somebody else.

LEWIS: The one who wrote the poems.

WARNIE: Ah? You're a poet, Mrs. Gresham?

JOY: Major Lewis, I know what you're thinking. You're thinking, God save us, she's going to start reciting.

WARNIE: I hope I'm not so bad–mannered.

JOY: No poetry at teatime. I know my manners, too. But just to redeem myself a little, I must tell you that I did once win a national poetry award, which I shared with Robert Frost. You have heard of Robert Frost?

WARNIE: Yes. Absolutely.

JOY: But that's all in the past now.

LEWIS: Why is that?

JOY: Let's say, I've turned away from the mirror.

(LEWIS *is intrigued*)

LEWIS: The mirror? Do you mean the reflection of yourself, or the reflection of the world?

JOY: The one being vanity, which is bad, the other being Art, which is good?

LEWIS: Possibly.

JOY: I don't make that distinction. See yourself in the mirror, you're separate from yourself. See the world in the mirror, you're separate from the world. I don't want that separation any more.

LEWIS: I could argue that art has quite the opposite effect. Great art breaks through that separateness and lets us touch the very heart of reality.

JOY: Breaks through? That makes it sound as if art does all the work. I'd say we have to do the breaking through ourselves. Art teaches us how to know it when we see it, but art isn't it.

LEWIS: Oh, I see. Art is some sort of instruction manual for life, is it?

JOY: Hey! That's one of your favorite tricks, Mr. Lewis.

LEWIS: I beg your pardon?

JOY: You redescribe your opponent's argument with a dismissive image and you think you've dismissed the argument.

(LEWIS *is taken aback by her vigorous riposte, but he bows to the truth in her criticism*)

LEWIS: I stand corrected.

(DOUGLAS *reenters near the tea table and stares at the bell that summons the waiter, obviously wanting to ring it*)

DOUGLAS: Mom! Can I ring the bell?

JOY: No.

DOUGLAS: Can I have a glass of milk?

JOY: No, I really don't think we should take up any more of your time.

(All rise)

LEWIS: It's extremely kind of you to come all this way. Warnie, I really should settle up. (WARNIE *rings the bell*) Tell me, Mrs. Gresham, how long are you planning to be in England?

JOY: To the end of December.

LEWIS: Do you expect to be in Oxford again?

JOY: I don't know. I could be.

LEWIS: What do you say, Warnie? Could we rise to a pot of home–brewed tea?

WARNIE: I think we can manage that.

LEWIS: Given adequate warning, of course.

JOY: Thank you. I'd like that.

LEWIS: Well, I'd better see what the damage is.

(The waiter enters and LEWIS *goes to pay the bill)*

JOY: Major Lewis, I must rely on you to tell me if I take up too much of your brother's time.

WARNIE: I'm sure you have time pressures of your own, Mrs. Gresham.

JOY: Oh, sure. Some.

(WARNIE *and* JOY *make their way to the exit)*

JOY: Your brother has given me so much. Through his writing, I mean. I think it might surprise you to know just how much.

WARNIE: Mrs. Gresham, everything surprises me.

(They exit. LEWIS *is about to follow when he sees* DOUGLAS,*who is still hanging round the bell)*

LEWIS: Douglas, do you remember the bell in the book?

DOUGLAS: Yes. And the queen was sitting in a stone chair, and she was very beautiful, and she didn't move or even breathe. But she wasn't dead.

LEWIS: No. She was waiting.

DOUGLAS: Waiting for someone to ring the bell.

LEWIS: Do you remember the writing on the pillar beneath the bell? "Make your choice, adventurous stranger. Strike the bell, and bide the danger."

(Music begins: the music of the magic world)

DOUGLAS: Can I?

LEWIS: It'll break the spell. It'll wake the queen.

DOUGLAS: I don't care.

LEWIS: Alright, then.

(DOUGLAS *rings the bell. The lights change. The screen rises. The door of the giant wardrobe slowly opens, to reveal a magical infinite space beyond: a child's vision of paradise.* DOUGLAS *walks towards the opening wardrobe door, as if hypnotised.* LEWIS *watches.* DOUGLAS *enters the magic world and the great door closes behind him. The music fades. The brief glimpse of another world is over. The lights change again. The set is once more the study at the Kilns.* WARNIE *enters, carrying Christmas paper chains.* LEWIS *joins him and together they hang the paper chains)*

WARNIE: Here you are, Jack.

LEWIS: Thank you, Warnie. It's only a cup of tea, Warnie. She won't stay long.

WARNIE: I didn't say a word.

(They work in silence for a few moments)

LEWIS: At least one can talk to her.

WARNIE: Listen to her.

LEWIS: You think she's going to make a nuisance of herself, don't you?

WARNIE: I'm sure you know what you're doing, Jack.

LEWIS: She sails back to New York at the end of the month. One can be so much more friendly to people who can't stay long.

WARNIE: What about the boy? What did you write in his book, by the way?

LEWIS: "The magic never ends."

WARNIE: You don't think that's overstating things a little?

LEWIS: He's only a child.

WARNIE: He'll ask for his money back later.

LEWIS: You know what she said about Douglas, how "It isn't true" is his way of saying "I want it to be true"? Don't you think that was perceptive?

WARNIE: I wonder what her husband thinks of her running round England like this.

LEWIS: This isn't the middle ages, Warnie.

WARNIE: She is American, of course.

LEWIS: And a poet.

WARNIE: She'll make you listen to one of her poems. I bet you ten shillings to sixpence. Then she'll say to you, "How do you like it, Mr. Lewis?" And you'll be stumped.

LEWIS: I shall say, "Only you could have written that."

WARNIE: "A distinctive voice."

(The doorbell rings)

LEWIS: Absolutely. There they are.

WARNIE: Is it a three–line whip?

LEWIS: Not at all.

(LEWIS *exits and can be heard greeting* JOY *and* DOUGLAS *offstage.* WARNIE *finishes the decorations)*

LEWIS: You found us. Welcome.

JOY: Hello! Take your coat off, Douglas. (JOY *enters and looks round, openly curious)* Hello. Oh, look at that.

(DOUGLAS, *following her, goes straight to a book-case and starts taking out books.* LEWIS *too enters)*

WARNIE: Mrs. Gresham, if you'll excuse me. I'm going to leave Jack to entertain you.

JOY: Oh. Good to see you again, Major Lewis. *(to* LEWIS) Do you mind Douglas looking at your books?

LEWIS: That's what books are for.

WARNIE: Jack is particularly hoping you'll introduce him to your poetry.

(WARNIE *gives* LEWIS *a private, meaning look, and exits)*

JOY: Are you?

LEWIS: I'd be interested to know what you write.

JOY: Wrote. All in the past. *(She takes off her hat, coat and gloves, and walks round the room examining it in more detail.* DOUGLAS *has curled up in a corner with a book)* How long have you and your brother lived here?

LEWIS: Would you believe, for over twenty years.

JOY: Good heavens! No wonder it's so comfortable.

LEWIS: My friends call it the Midden. They say if I
move the bookcases, the walls will fall down. Make
yourself at home and I'll see if I can summon up
some tea.

(He exits to get the tea)

JOY: What have you got there?

DOUGLAS: *The Lion, the Witch, and the Wardrobe.*

JOY: The best. Be careful with that. It's probably Mr.
Lewis' first copy.

(JOY *goes to his desk, to examine the books piled
there.* LEWIS *reenters with a tray of tea)*

LEWIS: As you see, I'm all prepared.

JOY: Sir Philip Sidney. Sir Thomas Wyatt. You like
your poets to have titles.

LEWIS: I'm working on "English Literature in the
Sixteenth Century, Excluding Drama." For
OHEL.

JOY: Oh hell?

LEWIS: The Oxford History of English Literature.

JOY: Sixteenth century. You got the easy one.

LEWIS: You think so?

JOY: Well, who is there? Spenser. If you cheat, you can squeeze Shakespeare in at the end.

LEWIS: Excluding drama.

JOY: "Venus and Adonis"? "The Rape of Lucrece"? They must be fifteen–ninety–something.

LEWIS: You're quite right.

JOY: Of course, you do have Knox's "The First Blast of the Trumpet Against the Monstrous Regiment of Women." That is what I call one hell of a title.

LEWIS: Do you really? And what did you call your book of poems?

JOY: *Letters to a Comrade.*

(She mimes an exaggerated yawn)

LEWIS: Do you remember any of them?

JOY: Oh, you don't want to hear—

LEWIS: No, no. Come on. Up you go.

JOY: Okay, let's get it over with. Let's see. Here's one I wrote when I was twenty–two. Spanish Civil War. It's called "Snow in Madrid."

LEWIS: In your own time.

(She recites, a little self-consciously, watching his reaction as she does so)

JOY: Softly, so casual,
Lovely, so light, so light.
The cruel sky lets fall
Something one does not fight.

Men before perishing
See with unwounding eye
For once, a gentle thing
Fall from the sky.

(LEWIS *says nothing. It is not what he expected)*

Embarrassed, huh? Well, buddy, you asked for it, you get out of it.

LEWIS: No. I'm touched.

JOY: Touched? Okay, that'll do. That's about its level. When was I ever in Madrid? The answer is, never.

LEWIS: Personal experience isn't everything.

JOY: You don't think so?

LEWIS: I've never been to Madrid, but I know it's there.

JOY: How about Narnia? Ever been there?

LEWIS: Now that's an interesting question. I'm not sure. I suppose I've sent surrogates of myself there. Children.

JOY: Yourself as a child.

LEWIS: Something like that.

JOY: It is different when you feel something for yourself. And it's a lot different when it hurts.

LEWIS: Just because something hurts, it doesn't make it more true. Or even more significant.

JOY: No. I guess not.

LEWIS: Douglas. There's some orange squash and some fruit cake, if you want it. (DOUGLAS *takes the glass of squash and the cake*) I'm not saying pain is purposeless, or even neutral. Not at all. But to find meaning in pain, there has to be something else. Pain is a tool. If you like, pain is God's mega—

JOY: God's megaphone to rouse a deaf world.

LEWIS: How embarrassing. You know my writing too well.

JOY: I know it because I've read it and reread it. I knew you pretty well before we met.

LEWIS: Ah, but you had not had the Personal Experience.

JOY: Mr. Lewis—listen, I can't go on calling you Mr. Lewis, it makes me feel like a kid. Can I call you Jack?

LEWIS: Of course you can.

JOY: Jack. I'm Joy.

(She shakes his hand)

LEWIS: Hello Joy. How do you do. Well, there . . . that's that.

JOY: So—Jack. Have you ever been really hurt?

LEWIS: You don't give up, do you?

JOY: I'm sorry. I withdraw the question. What do you do for Christmas?

LEWIS: Oh, much as last year. Roast turkey, Christmas pud, far too much to drink. How about you?

JOY: We haven't decided. Some lucky English hotel. That should be a new experience.

LEWIS: Then home for the New Year.

JOY: Home. Yes.

(This thought quietens JOY. There follows a short silence)

LEWIS: I have been really hurt, you know. The first time is always the worst. That was when my mother died.

JOY: How old were you?

LEWIS: Eight.

JOY: Old enough to hurt.

LEWIS: Oh yes. It was the end of my world. I remember my father in tears. Voices all over the house. Doors shutting and opening. It was a big house, all long, empty corridors. I remember I had the toothache. I wanted my mother to come to me. I cried for her to come, but she didn't come.

JOY: What was it?

LEWIS: It was cancer. It followed the usual course. An operation. An apparent recovery. A return of the disease. Increasing pain. Death.

JOY: And after death? Did you believe in heaven, when you were a child? Did you believe you'd meet her again?

LEWIS: No. She was gone. That was all.

JOY: And you went somewhere secret to cry?

LEWIS: I went somewhere secret. I didn't cry. *(They both fall silent again.* JOY, *feeling she has come close to him, is about to continue at this more per-*

sonal level, when he turns away) Douglas. There's
some more orange squash, if you'd like.

JOY: No thanks, Jack. We should go.

LEWIS: . . . Go? You only just got here. Well, I'm
frightfully glad you both came.

JOY: I'm frightfully glad you asked us. *(She rises)*
Douglas. Book back. Coat on.

(DOUGLAS *does as he is told)*

LEWIS: He doesn't make a fuss, does he?

JOY: Douglas and I understand each other.

LEWIS: Joy, I don't like to think of you Christmassing
in a hotel. Why don't you both come here? You'd
be very welcome.

JOY: No, no. You don't want strangers rampaging all
over your house.

LEWIS: I'll have to ask Warnie, of course. But speaking for myself, I would welcome the company.

JOY: It's very kind of you, Jack. You ask Warnie. But
we can look after ourselves, I promise you. We're
very independent, aren't we, Douglas?

(JOY *and* DOUGLAS *exit as they speak.* LEWIS *follows, speaking as he too exits)*

LEWIS: You'd be doing me a kindness. I'm sure Warnie will be delighted.

(WARNIE, RILEY, OAKLEY *and* HARRINGTON *enter, all carrying glasses. This is a pre–Christmas drinks party.* RILEY *gazes at the Christmas decorations.* LEWIS *reenters with a plate of cocktail sausages)*

RILEY: What I resent about Christmas is the general presumption of good will. I feel no good will towards my fellow men. I feel ill will.

LEWIS: It's got nothing to do with how you feel, Christopher. Feelings are far too unreliable.

RILEY: Maybe so, Jack, but they're very close to me. I'm very attached to my feelings. I won't hear a word against them. They're easily hurt.

HARRINGTON: I'm afraid Christmas is something of a lost cause, Jack.

LEWIS: That depends on how it's presented. If you tell people it's about peace in the world, and being kind to the poor and needy, then naturally nobody listens.

RILEY: Aha, the arch communicator in action. Give us the sales pitch, Jack.

LEWIS: Virgin Has Sex With Omnipotent Alien. Gives Birth to God.

RILEY: I've always thought the incarnation proves that God has a severely limited intellect. Who'd choose, voluntarily, to be human, when you have the option of staying safely divine?

LEWIS: Think of the magic, Christopher. The birth of a helpless, squealing creature who is also God. An all–powerful baby. Doesn't that satisfy your taste for the peculiar? It's the coming of new life in the heart of winter, when all the land is dead. The snow falls, and the trees are bare. All but one tree, which bears fruit. That's real magic.

HARRINGTON: I think you're a little hard on the poor and needy, Jack. No room at the inn, remember?

WARNIE: Jack's invited them to stay with us.

RILEY: Really, Jack?

HARRINGTON: Who?

WARNIE: Mother and child. They're upstairs.

LEWIS: Mrs. Gresham and her son. They're spending Christmas with us.

RILEY: Well, Jack, you have succeeded in surprising me. Who is Mrs. Gresham?

LEWIS: Wait and see.

WARNIE: She's an American.

RILEY: Curiouser and curiouser.

(JOY *enters*)

JOY: Merry Christmas!

LEWIS: Ah, Joy. Let me introduce you. Dr. Maurice Oakley. The Reverend Harry Harrington. Professor Christopher Riley. Mrs. Joy Gresham.

HARRINGTON: Delighted to meet you, Mrs. Gresham.

RILEY: Mrs. Gresham, how opportune. I understand you're from the United States of America.

JOY: Yes, I am.

RILEY: Then perhaps you can satisfy my curiosity on a small matter. Jack's children's stories are published in America, they tell me. Are they or are they not in translation?

JOY: I don't understand.

RILEY: *The Lion, the Witch, and the Clothes–Closet?*

LEWIS: Behave yourself, Christopher.

RILEY: Forgive me, Jack. Success breeds envy, as ever.

LEWIS: I don't know what you call success. Most of my friends treat my children's books as a form of juvenile dementia.

JOY: Have you read any of them, Professor Riley?

RILEY: Jack has read extracts aloud to me. It is one of his tests of friendship.

JOY: He's been reading me Sir Philip Sidney.

RILEY: Is that more bearable?

JOY: Bearable? Sidney's glorious.

(Her unselfconscious enthusiasm clearly delights LEWIS)

LEWIS: He is, isn't he?

JOY: He has this inspired image of Desire, capital D, as a baby that won't stop bawling. "Sleep, baby mine, Desire, Nurse Beauty singeth—"

LEWIS: "Thy cries, O baby, set mine head on aching." I'm afraid Sidney was rather down on desire.

JOY: Babies just yell until they get what they want. That's what I love about the image. It's precise. Nowadays, poets are so lazy.

LEWIS: You sound like me, Joy. You're supposed to be dragging me kicking into the twentieth century.

JOY: I've been force–feeding Jack T. S. Eliot, but even Eliot can be lazy. "When the evening is spread out against the sky, Like a patient etherised upon a table." What kind of image is that? He could just as easily have written, "Like a cocktail sausage upon a tray."

(RILEY *is beginning to feel excluded*)

RILEY: Congratulations, Jack. You seem to have found a soul mate.

LEWIS: I thought you believed we didn't have souls, Christopher.

RILEY: Well now, you see, I regard the soul as an essentially feminine accessory. "Anima." Quite different from "animus," the male variant. This is how I explain the otherwise puzzling difference between the sexes. Where men have intellect, women have soul.

JOY: Professor Riley, as you know, I'm an American and different cultures have different modes of discourse. I need a little guidance here. Are you being offensive, or merely stupid?

(LEWIS, HARRINGTON, OAKLEY, *and* WARNIE *laugh.* RILEY *pulls a face at* LEWIS, *rather put out, but trying to laugh it off*)

LEWIS: Serves you right, Christopher. Don't be such a bully.

RILEY: I feel like calling for police protection. Where on earth did you find her?

HARRINGTON: Tell me, Mrs. Gresham, how do you find England?

JOY: Cold. Dull.

RILEY: How very perceptive. How original.

JOY: And I don't much care for the weather, either. Will you excuse me, Jack? Revere and Harrington, Dr. Oakley, Professor Riley, it's been my pleasure.

(JOY *leaves them, but does not exit. She goes into the outer set, which we understand is another room, and there rereads an air–mail letter that arrived earlier in the day. Her brisk departure has the effect of breaking up the little party.* LEWIS *takes up the plate of cocktail sausages)*

LEWIS: Oh come on, let's finish these up, shall we?

HARRINGTON: I don't think I could, Jack.

WARNIE: I'll take those, Jack. We'll heat them up for supper.

(WARNIE *exits)*

LEWIS: I shall look forward to that.

(RILEY *takes* LEWIS *aside)*

RILEY: Jack, she's simply ghastly. You must get rid of her.

LEWIS: Oh come off it, Christopher. Just because she bit you back.

RILEY: Good Lord, I don't mind that. But she's got her hooks into you. You must see that.

LEWIS: Christopher, she's a married woman and she's a committed Christian. That may not warm the cockles of your heathen heart, but it does mean she's unlikely to have adulterous designs on me.

RILEY: Never send to know for whom the wedding bell tolls, Jack.

LEWIS: Look at you. All worked up over nothing. Fear not, she's harmless. And after Christmas, she sails back to New York.

RILEY: Beware Christmas, Jack. Look what happened to Scrooge.

LEWIS: Happy Christmas, Christopher.

RILEY: Easy to say, Jack. Easy to say.

(RILEY *exits*)

HARRINGTON: Thanks for the drinks Jack. Happy Christmas.

LEWIS: Are you off? Happy Christmas, Harry.

OAKLEY: Happy Christmas, Jack.

LEWIS: Good night, Maurice.

(HARRINGTON *and* OAKLEY *exit.* LEWIS *crosses the stage to join* JOY, *as she stands reading her letter*)

LEWIS: You mustn't mind about Christopher. It's nothing personal. Just how he is.

JOY: It's not important.

(LEWIS *realizes that something in her letter is absorbing her attention*)

LEWIS: Letter from home?

JOY: Yes.

LEWIS: Bad news?

JOY: In a way.

LEWIS: Anything I can do?

JOY: I'm not sure.

(She falls silent)

LEWIS: What is it?

JOY: If I was back home and this was happening, I'd write to you to tell me what to do. I could say it in a letter.

LEWIS: That's easy.

(He takes a chair and turns it so that its back is to JOY. *Then he sits where she can't see him)*

LEWIS: Tell me like a letter. Off you go. Dear Mr. Lewis . . .

(JOY falls in with his suggestion, at first tentatively, then with increasing feeling and fluency)

JOY: Dear Mr. Lewis. My husband has just written to me to tell me that he's fallen in love with another woman. Her name is Renée. He wants me to give him a divorce, so that he'll be free to marry her. *(She takes up the letter and reads from it)* "Renée and I are in love and have been since about the middle of August. If it had not been for our love I could not have come through this summer with as little anguish as I have, for things have been rough financially." Maybe you wonder if I knew about Renée. The answer is no. But Renée is not the first.

LEWIS: Do you love your husband?

JOY: I don't know how to answer that one. Bill's very talented, he wants to do right by everyone, he's a good man at heart and I guess I love him. Bill's a drunk, he sleeps around a lot, he's sometimes violent and I guess I haven't loved him for years. Once he broke a bottle over Douglas' head. Two days later he said, "When have you ever known me do an unkind thing?" He's worn me out. That's the truth of it. The only thing that's new is he wants a divorce.

LEWIS: I had no idea.

JOY: How could you? People never know about other people's lives. You have to live it to know it. Sorry. You don't agree with that.

LEWIS: Contrary to popular opinion, I don't know everything.

(JOY *recovers herself slowly*)

JOY: A lot of good things have come out of my life with Bill. We were happy at the beginning. And there's Douglas. And there's something else, too. Something that happened to me, that was very important, that in a strange way I owe to Bill. Something I don't talk about. But I'd like to tell you. If you don't mind.

LEWIS: Tell me.

JOY: It only lasted thirty seconds, maybe less, but it changed everything for me. I've been turning into a different person ever since.

LEWIS: What happened?

JOY: We were living in Westchester County. Bill was working in the city. One day he phoned from his office to say he was losing control of his mind and that he wasn't ever coming home. Bang went the

phone down. That was it. I had a small baby. I was
alone. I had no idea what to do. I phoned everyone
I knew. They hadn't seen Bill. I put the baby to bed
and I waited. He didn't come. I didn't know if he
was dead or alive. Round about midnight, I broke
down. I never felt so helpless in my life. The baby
was upstairs asleep. I was downstairs. I was crying.
Then there was someone else in the room. Just for
a few seconds, maybe half a minute. But I knew it
was a real person. More real than real. So real that
everything else was like shadows. I said something,
I've no idea what. I guess I was just saying, "Okay
then. Okay."

(She looks up at LEWIS *and sees that he understands)*

LEWIS: And tell me, what news of your husband?

JOY: Bill came home three days later. I told him. He
said, "I wish God would come to me." I'll say this
for Bill, he has an open mind. He just can't keep
any one thing in it for long.

LEWIS: Are you going to go back?

JOY: What about the divorce, Jack?

LEWIS: Marriage isn't just a legal contract.

JOY: We'd still be married, in the eyes of God.

LEWIS: Yes.

JOY: And I wouldn't be free to marry anyone else.

LEWIS: No.

JOY: No, I know. I've read your writings on the subject. Many times.

(LEWIS *says nothing. He can't tell her what she wants to hear*)

JOY: So, that's it, I guess.

LEWIS: Joy, tell me. Is this woman actually living with your husband in your house.

JOY: Yes. I guess so.

LEWIS: And that's where you're going back to?

JOY: Where else can I go?

LEWIS: And later?

JOY: I don't know. I'm sorry to burden you with all this. It's not your problem. Don't worry. I'll be alright. I always have been.

LEWIS: I wish there was some way I could help.

JOY: There is.

(*He looks up, almost frightened to hear what she has to say*)

LEWIS: Yes?

JOY: Be my friend.

LEWIS: Well, I'm that already.

JOY: I know. Thank you. I'm just going to go upstairs now . . .

(On the point of further tears, JOY *hurries out.* LEWIS *looks after her, for a moment or two. Then he too rises and exits, in a different direction. The lighting changes. It is morning.* WARNIE *enters, carrying the breakfast tray as he did earlier, and his newspaper. He pours out two cups of coffee.* LEWIS *enters, carrying the morning mail)*

WARNIE: Morning, Jack.

LEWIS: Morning. Two for you.

(He sits at his desk. The bachelor routine has returned. After a while, and without taking their eyes off their reading, they have one of their noncommittal conversations)

WARNIE: You miss her, don't you?

LEWIS: Things are quieter now.

WARNIE: I'm afraid I'm not much of a talker.

LEWIS: One of your many virtues, Warnie.

WARNIE: Is she coming back?

LEWIS: No, no. Why should she come back? *(An interval of silence)* I haven't really thanked you, Warnie.

WARNIE: What for?

LEWIS: You've been very tolerant. Very considerate.

WARNIE: Any friend of yours, Jack.

LEWIS: I know. *(The doorbell rings.* LEWIS *calls out, without rising, or even turning his attention from what he is writing)* That'll be Christopher. Door's open, Christopher.

(WARNIE *looks at his watch, a little surprised at this early visit, and then goes back to reading the paper.* RILEY *enters, carrying a typescript. He looks round with mock trepidation)*

RILEY: Is it safe to come in? *La belle* dame *sans merci?*

(He pronounces "dame" in the American manner)

LEWIS: Now Christopher, you know perfectly well that she went back to New York ages ago.

(RILEY *puts the typescript on* LEWIS' *desk before him)*

RILEY: Tom's latest, as promised. The only copy.

LEWIS: Is it up to scratch?

RILEY: Not bad. If he wasn't a friend, I'd say pretty good.

(He goes to WARNIE)

RILEY: Morning, Warnie.

WARNIE: Morning, Christopher.

(RILEY *turns and remarks to* LEWIS)

RILEY: Just as well, perhaps, Jack.

LEWIS: What is?

RILEY: The return of the native.

LEWIS: What are you trying to say?

RILEY: You know how people talk.

LEWIS: To be honest, Christopher, I don't know and I don't care. A like–minded man and woman are entitled to be friends, it seems to me. I don't see why I should disqualify half the human race just because they're also available for other purposes.

RILEY: I won't quarrel with that. Friendship for ever.

LEWIS: It's all love or sex these days. Friendship is almost as quaint and outdated a notion as chastity.

Soon friends will be like the elves and the pixies; fabulous mythical creatures from a distant past.

RILEY: Too optimistic, Jack. Friendship will be made illegal, clearly. 'The accused has been found guilty of gross public friendship. I hereby pass sentence of five years marriage, with no remission.'

(They chuckle. WARNIE *puts down his paper and rises from his chair)*

WARNIE: No news, of course. Never is.

RILEY: Shall we see you in hall, Warnie? Like old times?

WARNIE: Like old times, Christopher. Why not?

*(*WARNIE *exits.* RILEY *sits down in his chair and picks up the newspaper.* LEWIS *becomes reflective)*

LEWIS: Tell me something, Christopher. How can I put this? Would you say that you were . . . content?

RILEY: I am as I am. The world is as it is. My contentment or otherwise has very little to do with it.

LEWIS: You don't ever feel a sense of waste?

RILEY: Of course. All life is waste. Remember, I don't have your faith in divine recycling.

LEWIS: I've always found this a trying time of the year. The leaves not yet out. Mud everywhere you go. The frosty mornings gone and the sunny mornings not yet come. The air dank and unhealthy. Give me blizzards and frozen pipes, but not this nothing time. Not this waiting room of a world.

RILEY: May will come, Jack. And June. And July.

LEWIS: And I have two books to finish and six talks to write and letters, letters, letters.

(He turns to his work, waiting on his desk. RILEY *rises from his chair and watches him with some sympathy, understanding him better than his friend realises. Then he exits.* LEWIS *finds it difficult to concentrate, but after a few moments, he gets into the way of it. As he works,* JOY *enters. He does not see her. She stands still, watching* LEWIS *work, but does not speak.* LEWIS *becomes aware that he is not alone. He raises his head, listening without turning round)*

JOY: Remember me, Jack?

LEWIS: Joy! *(He turns round and sees her)* What are you doing here?

JOY: The door was open.

LEWIS: But . . . ?

JOY: We live here now. Douglas and I.

LEWIS: Here? In Oxford?

JOY: Yes, but don't worry. We have our own house. We'll be no trouble at all.

(LEWIS *stares at her, still too stunned to be polite*)

JOY: Want a cup of tea?

LEWIS: Yes. Thank you very much. I'd love one.

JOY: Then you're going to have to make it. This is your house.

LEWIS: Of course. Yes. I'm sorry, Joy, I'm a little confused. Why didn't you write?

JOY: What for? To ask permission?

LEWIS: No, no. But . . . when did you decide this? How did you find a house? How was it all arranged?

JOY: And what have I done with Bill? We're divorced. No more Bill. No more America.

LEWIS: I see.

JOY: Do you mind?

LEWIS: Why should I mind?

JOY: I don't know. You might.

LEWIS: No. I don't mind.

JOY: That's alright, then. *(They walk forward, out of the study. The screen falls)* So tell me the news.

LEWIS: What news?

JOY: Don't tell me that time has stood still since I've been away.

LEWIS: Gone by at a slow amble, perhaps. I may be offered a chair at Cambridge, if you call that news. Professor of Medieval and Renaissance Literature.

JOY: Will you take it?

LEWIS: Probably.

JOY: You'd leave Oxford?

LEWIS: Only to teach. I'd go on living here. Cambridge is a chilly sort of town.

JOY: So you won't be moving out just as I move in?

(She makes a joke of this, but she is secretly relieved that he is not leaving Oxford. He looks at her with affection)

LEWIS: I really am very—very surprised to see you, you know.

JOY: I think you're overdoing the surprise a bit, Jack. I wasn't dead. I was only in America.

LEWIS: Yes, of course. But you see, I've been thinking about—*(He hesitates to say it; then decides he
will)* Oh, alright, I've been thinking about you.

JOY: I am honored.

LEWIS: There we are. I was thinking about you. And
all of a sudden there you were.

JOY: Here I am. Present tense. Present and tense.

LEWIS: I really am very glad to see you again, Joy.

JOY: Thank you, Jack.

*(He has gone a little further than he intended and
changes the subject to the safer, more neutral matter now facing them)*

LEWIS: Moving house is a sort of revolution, I always
think. The old order is overthrown, a new order
waits to be born. One wakes up facing a strange
way, one's books are all in strange places and
there's nowhere to hang one's dressing gown.

*(In the course of this speech, the screen rises to
reveal* JOY's *house. It is empty but for packing
cases)*

JOY: When did you last move house?

LEWIS: Twenty–five years ago. Thank God that's
over.

(JOY *laughs. She goes to work on the packing cases.*
LEWIS *looks about the room)*

JOY: I don't know why I brought all this stuff.

LEWIS: What is it?

JOY: My uncollected works. How can I have written
all this stuff?

LEWIS: I'm sure it's nothing to be ashamed of.

JOY: You haven't read it. Nor will you.

LEWIS: What can I do to help?

JOY: Books into shelves.

LEWIS: Books into shelves. Any particular order?

JOY: Put them anywhere they'll fit. I'll sort them out
later. (LEWIS *takes the books and starts reading one
of them.* JOY *watches him)* Jack, are you sure you
want to do this?

LEWIS: I said I'd help. *(They work on in silence for a
few moments)* Joy, how does Bill feel about you
coming to live in England?

JOY: I don't think he likes it. On the other hand, he
can only afford to give me sixty dollars a month and
England's cheaper.

LEWIS: How much is that? It doesn't sound enough.

JOY: We'll manage.

LEWIS: If you find things are getting tight, you will let me know, won't you?

JOY: I don't want to take your money, Jack.

LEWIS: Don't be silly. That's what friends are for.

JOY: We are friends, aren't we?

LEWIS: We most certainly are.

(JOY's *attention is caught by a newspaper in which her possessions have been packed. The headline announces Princess Margaret's dramatic 'duty before love' decision not to marry Group–Captain Peter Townsend)*

JOY: "Should Princess Margaret have followed the dictates of her heart? Group–Captain Peter Townsend's lips are sealed, but his hands are shaking. She chose duty before love." So what do you think about the heartbreak princess?

LEWIS: The dictates of her heart! It almost sounds like a higher authority, doesn't it? All it means is, doing what she feels like doing.

JOY: I knew you'd be on the side of duty.

LEWIS: I don't pretend it's an easy decision.

JOY: Easy it's not.

(She returns to the business of unpacking)

LEWIS: It's a big change for you, this.

JOY: England?

LEWIS: Yes.

JOY: If it turns out to be a mistake, I'll have lost very little. But I do hope it works out for Douglas.

LEWIS: What made you decide?

JOY: I had to go somewhere. And I like England.

LEWIS: And it's cheaper.

JOY: I like Oxford.

LEWIS: All those warmhearted dons, with their love of female company.

JOY: I can handle that.

LEWIS: The balmy English weather.

JOY: I like the way Oxford's been here a long time. Not everything is the impulse of the moment. I like being among educated people. And I like living in the same town as you. Do you mind?

LEWIS: My dear Joy, I don't own Oxford.

JOY: Do you mind?

LEWIS: Of course I don't mind. Why should I?

JOY: You know what I mean, Jack.

LEWIS: I'm delighted to have you as a neighbor. *(She looks at him)* Why are you looking at me like that?

JOY: Like what?

LEWIS: As if I'm lying to you. Why should I lie to you? I mean what I say.

JOY: I know that. But you don't say it all, do you?

LEWIS: One can't say it all. It would take too long.

JOY: Alright, Jack. But I trust you to tell me anything I need to know.

(Again, she returns to the unpacking. LEWIS *puzzles over what she has just said)*

LEWIS: What sort of thing do you need to know?

JOY: I want to stay friends with you, Jack. I need to know anything that would make that hard for you.

LEWIS: I see.

JOY: We might as well know where we are.

LEWIS: Best to have things out in the open, you think?

LEWIS: Good evening. The subject of my talk tonight is love, pain and suffering. Of course, as a comfortably-situated middle-aged bachelor, I must be quite an authority on pain and love, wouldn't you have thought.

Nigel Hawthorne as Jack Lewis in the 1990 U.S. production at the Brooks Atkinson Theatre, New York City.

Photo by Martha Swope.

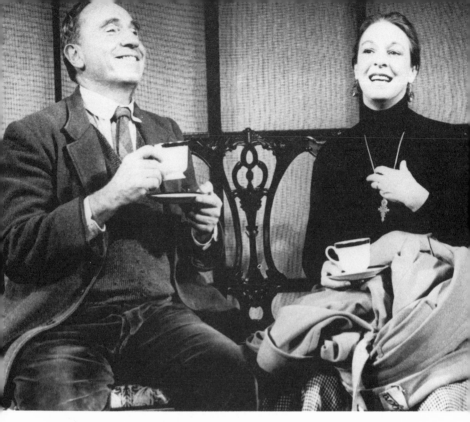

JOY: It's kind of you to find time to meet me. So many people must write you. You can't forever be having tea with strange women.

LEWIS: Not completely strange, Mrs. Gresham. I've enjoyed our correspondence.

JOY: Enjoyed? Okay.

LEWIS: Not the word you would use?

JOY: Your letters have been the most important thing in my life.

LEWIS: Oh dear.

JOY: But let's pretend I didn't say that. This is tea. This is England.

Jane Alexander, at right, as Joy with Nigel Hawthorne as Jack in the 1990 U.S. production at the Brooks Atkinson Theatre, New York City.
Photo by Martha Swope.

JOY: I've been force-feeding Jack T.S. Eliot, but even Eliot can be lazy....
RILEY: Congratulations, Jack. You seem to have found a soul mate.... I regard the soul as an essentially feminine accessory.... Where men have intellect, women have soul.
JOY: Professor Riley, as you know, I'm an American and different cultures have different modes of discourse. I need a little guidance here. Are you being offensive, or merely stupid?

Jane Alexander as Joy Davidman in the 1990 U.S. production at the Brooks Atkinson Theatre, New York City.
Photo by Martha Swope.

JOY: You just don't know how to be in the sun. . . . Now put that face of yours up here. Feel it on your face. The sun so close you could stick out your tongue and lick it. No words. No thoughts. Just the sun on your face. The sound of the wind in the olive trees, and the cicadas. . . . In this land, nothing is impossible. Nothing is forbidden. You could even take off your coat.

Jane Alexander, seated at left, as Joy with Nigel Hawthorne as Jack in the 1990 U.S. production at the Brooks Atkinson Theatre, New York City. *Photo by Martha Swope.*

JOY: That's how I like it.

LEWIS: You never can really tell what's going on between people, can you? People jump to conclusions. Sometimes it makes me quite angry the way people aren't allowed to be . . . well, just friends.

JOY: Like us, you mean.

LEWIS: Like us. I don't mean to say that friendship is a small thing. As a matter of fact, I rate it as one of this life's most precious gifts.

JOY: But . . .

LEWIS: But it shouldn't be turned into a watered–down version of something it is not.

JOY: Such as . . .

LEWIS: Such as, well, to give you one example, romantic love. Which nowadays is just about the only emotion men and women are permitted to feel for each other. Though that's not to say that friendship isn't, in its way—

JOY: A kind of love.

LEWIS: A kind of love. I knew you'd understand.

JOY: I understand better than that, Jack. You are a bachelor and I am a divorced woman. Some people might suppose you to have some idea of marrying me. You have no such idea. I am to have no false expectations. You want to have this "out in the open" because you care about me and don't want me to be hurt. Have I understood you correctly?

LEWIS: You are extraordinary. I really don't know what to say.

JOY: It's okay. I just said it. Wasn't so hard, was it?

LEWIS: I'm not used to this . . . whatever it is.

JOY: Naming names. That's all it is.

LEWIS: Yes.

JOY: So now you don't need to be afraid of me, do you?

LEWIS: Good Lord, I was never afraid of you, Joy.

(She looks at him. He shrugs and smiles)

JOY: I really do appreciate your help, Jack.

LEWIS: The least I can do. Look, I'm sure there are far more substantial ways I can help, that you're not telling me about.

JOY: I don't want to exhaust your good will.

LEWIS: No fear of that. I think it grows by being drawn on.

JOY: There is something you could do which would help me enormously. But if I ask for something and you can't give it, I want you to just say no. I mean, just, no. No guilt, no evasion, no running away.

LEWIS: I hope so. I don't think you'd ask for anything beyond my power to give.

JOY: No. It's not beyond your power to give . . .

LEWIS: So, there's something in particular, isn't there?

JOY: Yes, there is. There is something you could do that would help me a great deal.

LEWIS: I think I know what it is. You want me to put the kettle on.

(JOY *laughs*)

JOY: Come on, I'll tell you about it in the kitchen, you fox.

LEWIS: Fox? What do you mean, Fox?

(She exits. LEWIS exits. The screen falls. WARNIE enters with a deckchair and settles down to read. LEWIS enters with a deckchair of his own and does likewise. After a few moments)

WARNIE: So she's settled over here for good, has she?

LEWIS: Who knows? For the foreseeable future.

WARNIE: Why Oxford?

LEWIS: Why not Oxford? Dreaming spires and so forth.

WARNIE: You know how it looks, don't you, Jack?

LEWIS: I know.

(Neither of them have taken their noses out of their books. There follows a short silence. Then)

LEWIS: She's a good friend to me, Warnie. That's all.

(WARNIE nods)

WARNIE: Is that how she sees it?

LEWIS: I wouldn't presume to raise the matter.

WARNIE: No. Of course not.

(Another short silence)

LEWIS: Oh, Warnie. There is something you should know.

WARNIE: What's that, Jack?

LEWIS: I've agreed to marry her.

WARNIE: You have?

LEWIS: Yes. Seemed like the right thing to do.

WARNIE: You astound me. No, I mean . . .

LEWIS: It's alright, Warnie. Nothing's going to change. I'm not really going to marry Joy.

WARNIE: You're not?

LEWIS: What I have agreed to do is extend my British citizenship to her, so that she can go on living in England.

WARNIE: By marrying her.

LEWIS: Only technically.

WARNIE: You're marrying Joy technically?

LEWIS: A true marriage is a declaration before God, not before some government official. Joy will keep her own name. She will go on living in her own house. We will go on living here exactly as before. No one will even know the marriage has taken place, apart from you, Somerset House and the Department of Immigration. It is nothing more than a bureaucratic formality. See you at tea.

(A clap of thunder is heard)

WARNIE: Oh, blast.

(In the course of this speech, LEWIS rises, takes up his chair and at the end, exits. WARNIE exits. The screen rises to reveal a Registry Office, where JOY waits before a REGISTRAR. WARNIE joins them.

LEWIS *enters, hurriedly and late, carrying a pile of books)*

LEWIS: I'm so sorry.

REGISTRAR: Mr. Lewis. Please be seated. *(The* REGIS-TRAR *opens a book and reads from it)* We'll proceed at once. Before you are joined in matrimony, I have to remind you of the solemn and binding character of the vows you are about to make. Marriage according to the law of this country is the union of one man with one woman, voluntarily entered into for life, to the exclusion of all others. Now we proceed to the declarations. If you'd both stand. Mr. Lewis, if you'll repeat after me, "I call upon these persons here present."

(LEWIS *speaks in an unduly clear voice)*

LEWIS: I call upon these persons here present.

REGISTRAR: "To witness that I, Clive Staples Lewis."

LEWIS: To witness that I, Clive Staples Lewis.

REGISTRAR: "Do take thee, Helen Joy Davidman."

LEWIS: Do take thee, Helen Joy Davidman.

REGISTRAR: "To be my lawful wedded wife."

LEWIS: To be my lawful wedded wife.

REGISTRAR: Miss Davidman, if you'll repeat after me. "I call upon these persons here present."

(JOY's *responses are more muted*)

JOY: I call upon these persons here present.

REGISTRAR: "To witness that I, Helen Joy Davidman."

JOY: To witness that I, Helen Joy Davidman.

REGISTRAR: "Do take thee, Clive Staples Lewis."

JOY: Do take thee, Clive Staples Lewis.

REGISTRAR: "To be my lawful wedded husband."

JOY: To be my lawful wedded husband.

REGISTRAR: Do we have a ring?

(LEWIS *and* JOY *speak together*)

LEWIS AND JOY: No. Sorry.

(*The whole affair is very awkward and embarrassing*)

REGISTRAR: No ring. Very well. If you'll please both sign the register. Before you sign, be careful to check that all the details are exactly correct.

(JOY *signs the register quickly.* LEWIS *studies it carefully before signing*)

LEWIS: Let's see . . . Clive Staples Lewis . . . Helen Joy Davidman . . . Headington Quarry . . . April 23rd. That seems to be roughly in order. Well done.

(LEWIS *signs the register, as do* WARNIE, *a* WITNESS, *the* REGISTRAR, *and finally the* CLERK. *The* CLERK *puts the certificate in an envelope*)

CLERK: Mrs. Lewis. Mrs. Lewis.

(JOY *comes and takes the envelope*)

REGISTRAR: May I be the first to congratulate you and wish you every happiness in your life together.

LEWIS: Well, do you know, that's most kind of you. Good day.

(The REGISTRAR *exits.* LEWIS, JOY *and* WARNIE *walk downstage and the screen falls behind them. They have come out into rain)*

JOY: What a terrible day.

LEWIS: That's that, then.

JOY: Can I invite you both back for a drink?

LEWIS: I simply can't. I've got a lot of work to do. I really shouldn't be here at all.

JOY: Of course, Jack. Off you go.

(LEWIS *exits*)

WARNIE: I would be most grateful for a drink, Joy.

JOY: That's kind of you, Warnie. I must admit, I found that an unusual experience.

WARNIE: Yes. You must forgive Jack.

JOY: Oh, I'm getting to know him a little by now. I think I understand him. I'm very grateful to him.

WARNIE: Nobody is to know, he tells me.

JOY: That's right. Best that way.

WARNIE: What he actually said was, it will be as if it never happened.

JOY: Yes.

WARNIE: Odd business.

JOY: It is that.

WARNIE: Jack plays safe, you see. Always has.

JOY: I do rather need that drink.

(They exit. The screen rises to reveal JOY's *house.* LEWIS *is there with* DOUGLAS, *who is in his pyjamas)*

LEWIS: So how do you like it here?

DOUGLAS: Not much. Mom says we don't have to stay if we don't like it.

LEWIS: So you're seeing if you like it.

DOUGLAS: Except I don't.

LEWIS: What about your mother?

DOUGLAS: I guess she likes it.

LEWIS: And you want to stay with her?

DOUGLAS: Yes. Have you met my dad?

LEWIS: No.

DOUGLAS: He's okay, my dad. But I love Mom the best.

(JOY *enters*)

JOY: Douglas. Bed.

(DOUGLAS *turns to go*)

DOUGLAS: Night, Mr. Lewis.

LEWIS: Goodnight, Douglas.

JOY: One chapter.

(DOUGLAS *exits*)

LEWIS: He's so obedient. I like him.

JOY: He likes you.

LEWIS: He doesn't seem very impressed by England.

JOY: He'll get used to it.

LEWIS: So this is it, is it? Land of hope and glory?

JOY: I think so. I'm happier here than I've been in a long time.

LEWIS: That's good.

JOY: Mostly because of you, Jack. One good friend can make all the difference.

LEWIS: You're not getting sick of the sight of me?

JOY: Not yet. Though heaven knows what the neighbors think.

LEWIS: The worst, I've no doubt.

JOY: Don't you sometimes burst to share the joke?

LEWIS: What joke?

JOY: Well. Here's the neighbors thinking we're unmarried and up to all sorts of wickedness, while all along we're married and up to nothing at all.

LEWIS: I'd better be on my merry way.

(She sees that her joke makes him uneasy)

JOY: Only technically married, of course.

LEWIS: Oh, look. Do you think I come round too often?

JOY: Too often for what? We're friends. That's what we agreed. Good friends.

(LEWIS *prepares to leave. She gets his coat and helps him on with it. Her hands rest on his shoulders. He moves away)*

JOY: I'm not going to talk about it anymore. You get that twitchy look in your eyes and you start feeling in your coat pockets like there's something there you have to find.

(LEWIS *is doing just as she describes. He stops and removes his hands from his pockets)*

LEWIS: You know me too well.

JOY: Don't say that. Just say, I know you.

LEWIS: You know me.

DOUGLAS *(offstage):* Mom! I'm ready!

JOY: I'll be right there.

LEWIS: I'll say goodnight then.

(As LEWIS *leaves, a sudden pain strikes her)*

JOY: Ah!

LEWIS: What is it?

JOY: It's nothing. I just stumbled. I'm fine. See you soon.

LEWIS: Well, goodnight, then.

JOY: Goodnight, Jack.

(He pats her on one arm and they exchange a peck on the cheek. LEWIS *exits.* JOY *stands looking after him. Then she turns to go to* DOUGLAS. *Her body twists and her mouth opens in a silent scream. Suddenly, she crumples to the floor)*

Curtain.

ACT
TWO

ACT
TWO

ACT TWO

The screen is down. LEWIS *enters and speaks to the audience as he did at the beginning of the play. As the talk proceeds, there are signs that he is using it to persuade himself of a belief that is beginning to slide. However, at this stage, he hardly realises this process himself.*

LEWIS: Recently a friend of mine, a brave and Christian woman, collapsed in terrible pain. One minute she seemed fit and well. The next minute she was in agony. She is now in hospital, suffering from advanced bone cancer, and almost certainly dying. Why?

I find it hard to believe that God loves her. If you love someone, you don't want them to suffer. You can't bear it. You want to take their suffering onto yourself. If even I feel like that, why doesn't God? Not just once in history, on the cross, but again and again? Today. Now.

It's at times like this that we have to remind ourselves of the very core of the Christian faith. There are other worlds than this. This world, that seems so real, is no more than a shadow of the life to come. If we believe that all is well in this present life, if we can imagine nothing more satisfactory than this present life, then we are under a dangerous illusion. All is not well. Believe me, all is not well.

(His present experience, JOY's *suffering, breaks through the familiar pattern of his lecture)*

Suffering . . . by suffering . . . through suffering, we release our hold on the toys of this world, and know that our true good lies in another world.

But after we have suffered so much, must we still suffer more? And more?

(He has no answer to this question, which torments him. All he can do is repeat his familiar lines, wanting to believe them)

We are like blocks of stone, out of which the sculptor carves the forms of men. The blows of his chisel, which hurt us so much, are what make us perfect.

(He turns aside, to hide his feelings. WARNIE *enters with* DOUGLAS. *He sits* DOUGLAS *down on a chair and comes to* LEWIS. DOUGLAS *reads the book he is carrying)*

WARNIE: How is she?

LEWIS: Not good. Not good.

WARNIE: I'm sorry, Jack.

LEWIS: I want her to be well again, you see.

WARNIE: Of course you do. We all do.

LEWIS: What a dangerous world we live in, Warnie. How full of cutting edges. They give her morphine, you know. No morphine for me.

WARNIE: You've been up all night, Jack. You must get some sleep.

LEWIS: I can't sleep. I've never felt more awake in my life. *(He moves restlessly about)* You see, Warnie, this isn't the right time. It's too soon.

WARNIE: Too soon for what, Jack?

LEWIS: I haven't had time, you see, Warnie.

WARNIE: Time for what, Jack?

LEWIS: Time to talk. Time to get to know her. Time to . . . say things.

(Now WARNIE *understands)*

WARNIE: It doesn't take long.

LEWIS: No. I suppose not.

WARNIE: Whatever it is, I should just say it.

LEWIS: Would you, Warnie? You're quite right, of course. But it's difficult, you see.

WARNIE: Yes. I do see that.

LEWIS: I just want her to be well again. That's all.

(The screen rises, revealing a hospital room. JOY *lies in a bed. A* NURSE *comes forward to collect* DOUGLAS. LEWIS *goes to* DOUGLAS *to prepare him)* Douglas, you know she's not strong, don't you? But she's in very good hands. Very good hands. She sleeps a lot. You mustn't mind that. Sleep's good for her. Sleep, the great healer.

WARNIE: Are you a muffin man, Douglas? Like muffins, do you?

DOUGLAS: Yes.

WARNIE: We'll have a muffin tea later. I shall like that.

(The NURSE *takes* DOUGLAS *to* JOY'*s bedside)*

NURSE: Douglas, you can see your mother now.

LEWIS: Warnie, that's *The Magician's Nephew* he's carrying around with him.

WARNIE: Yes. I noticed.

LEWIS: The boy travels to Narnia, and picks a magic apple, and brings it back to his dying mother, and makes her well again.

WARNIE: Poor kid.

LEWIS: I'm a fraud, Warnie.

(A DOCTOR *enters and comes to* LEWIS*)*

DOCTOR: Mr. Lewis.

LEWIS: Ah, Doctor. Any change?

DOCTOR: She's been sleeping. Otherwise, nothing to report, really.

LEWIS: How much has she been told?

DOCTOR: She's been told that the cancer has eaten through her left femur. That she has a malignant tumor in one breast. She knows it's serious. How can she not know? Her hip bone snapped like a frozen twig.

LEWIS: So suddenly. I don't understand. How can this have happened with no warning?

DOCTOR: I'm told there had been occasional pain before.

LEWIS: Everyone has occasional pain.

DOCTOR: That's often how it goes, I'm afraid.

LEWIS: I just don't understand it.

DOCTOR: To tell you the truth, Mr. Lewis, nor do we.

WARNIE: How bad is it?

LEWIS: She's likely to die.

DOCTOR: That's putting it more starkly than I would choose. I don't pretend to be able to prophesy the future.

LEWIS: No. But it's true, isn't it?

DOCTOR: The cancer is very advanced.

(Inside the hospital room, DOUGLAS kisses his mother and leaves her. He comes out into the corridor)

LEWIS: Right. Thank you, Doctor.

(The DOCTOR exits. WARNIE takes charge of DOUGLAS)

WARNIE: Muffins. Muffins. That's what's needed. There's bound to be muffins somewhere.

(WARNIE and DOUGLAS exit. LEWIS walks on alone into the hospital room, where JOY lies in bed, weakened by pain and by painkillers)

LEWIS: Hello, Joy.

JOY: Hello, Jack.

LEWIS: How's the pain?

JOY: Kind of pushy.

LEWIS: Don't talk if it hurts.

JOY: Did you visit before?

LEWIS: Yes. A couple of times.

JOY: I thought so.

LEWIS: They're going to operate on the broken hip tomorrow.

JOY: I'm sorry, Jack. I didn't mean you to have all this bother.

LEWIS: Tush, woman. You're the one who's having the bother.

JOY: What I mean is, I don't expect you to worry about me.

LEWIS: Oh? And who do you expect to worry about you?

JOY: You know what I'm trying to say.

LEWIS: Who else should be worrying about you but me? You are my wife.

JOY: Technically.

LEWIS: Then I shall worry about you technically.

JOY: Just how much is there to worry about, Jack? They won't tell me.

LEWIS: That's because they're not sure themselves.

JOY: Tell me, Jack.

LEWIS: I don't know any more than they do, Joy.

JOY: Please.

LEWIS *(after a pause):* They expect you to die.

JOY: Thank you. *(Having got what she wanted, she pauses to regain strength. Then)* What do you say, Jack? I'm a Jew. Divorced. Broke. And I'm dying of cancer. Do I get a discount?

LEWIS: I don't want to lose you, Joy.

JOY: I don't want to be lost. You know something? You seem different. You look at me properly now.

LEWIS: Didn't I before?

JOY: Not properly.

LEWIS: Would you give me your hand?

(He holds out his hand again. This time she gives him her hand. He holds it and strokes it)

JOY: Can I say anything I want, Jack?

LEWIS: Yes.

JOY: Anything?

LEWIS: Yes.

JOY: You know it anyway.

LEWIS: Yes.

JOY: I'm still going to say it.

LEWIS: You say it.

JOY: I love you, Jack.

(He seems about to respond with a declaration of his own. But it does not quite come out)

LEWIS: Better now?

JOY: Better. Do you mind?

LEWIS: No.

(A spasm of pain passes through her. He watches JOY *in pain. He can't bear it. He goes looking for a* NURSE) Nurse! Nurse!

(A NURSE *enters and examines* JOY)

NURSE: I'll fetch the doctor.

(The NURSE *leaves.* LEWIS *holds* JOY's *hand as she suffers. The* DOCTOR *enters at last and comes to* JOY's *side. The screen falls.* LEWIS *exits.* HARRINGTON *and* RILEY *enter. They stroll across the stage together, gravely discussing their friend's situation)*

HARRINGTON: Poor Jack. It's knocked him completely off balance.

RILEY: Looks bad, does it?

HARRINGTON: Oh yes. They don't expect her to live.

RILEY: Sad business.

HARRINGTON: Has he said anything to you?

RILEY: About her?

HARRINGTON: Yes.

RILEY: No. Nothing.

(OAKLEY *crosses the stage*)

OAKLEY: Morning, Harry.

HARRINGTON: Morning, Maurice.

OAKLEY: Christopher.

RILEY: Maurice.

(OAKLEY *exits*)

HARRINGTON: I don't suppose you were listening in to the wireless last night?

RILEY: Jack wasn't on, was he?

HARRINGTON: No, no. It was *Twenty Questions.* You're not a Gilbert Harding appreciator, then?

RILEY: His fascination has eluded me so far.

HARRINGTON *(chuckling at the memory):* Oh, he's something quite tremendous. The other day he said, "When I hear the words 'ethical' and 'artistic,' I say fiddle–de–dee and tiddley–push."

RILEY: Ye–es. That is rather good.

(LEWIS *enters in a distracted state)*

HARRINGTON: Do you listen to *Twenty Questions,* Jack?

LEWIS: *Twenty Questions?* No. I can't say I do, Harry.

RILEY: Other things to think about, eh, Jack?

LEWIS: Other things. Yes. *(There is a short awkward pause. Neither* RILEY *nor* HARRINGTON *feel quite able to bring up the subject of* JOY. LEWIS *resolves the awkwardness by starting to speak of her, without introduction, as if she is as much in their minds as she is in his)* She's in very good hands. She sleeps a good deal. Sleep is good, don't you think? Sleep, the great healer.

HARRINGTON: Great healer.

RILEY: I'm so sorry about all this, Jack.

LEWIS: Yes. It's all come too soon, you see. Her affairs aren't in order. What's to happen to Douglas, for example?

HARRINGTON: I suppose his father—

LEWIS: She doesn't want that. He drinks, you see.

HARRINGTON: I don't really see what you can do about that.

LEWIS: Do you think I should take the boy in?

HARRINGTON: There must be relatives, Jack. I mean, it's not as if . . .

LEWIS: Not as if what?

HARRINGTON: Well, she's your friend, of course, but she's not . . . well, family.

LEWIS: Not my wife?

HARRINGTON *(giving a nervous laugh at such a prospect):* No. Of course not.

LEWIS: Of course not. Impossible. Unthinkable.

HARRINGTON: I only meant—

LEWIS: How could Joy be my wife? I'd have to love her, wouldn't I? I'd have to care more for her than for anyone else in this world. I'd have to be suffering the torments of the damned at the prospect of losing her.

HARRINGTON *(awed by* LEWIS*'s passionate outburst):* I'm sorry, Jack. I didn't know.

LEWIS: Nor did I, Harry. *(Suddenly, his manner changes. He becomes calm, almost businesslike)* I'm going to marry her, Harry. I've made up my mind. I want you to marry us properly, Harry, before God.

(HARRINGTON *is now embarrassed professionally as well as personally)*

HARRINGTON: I think it would be best if we talked about this later, Jack.

LEWIS: We don't have a later.

HARRINGTON: Still. It's not entirely plain sailing, is it?

(He looks to RILEY *for support)*

RILEY: I think Harry's trying to say it's against the rules.

HARRINGTON: She's a divorced woman, Jack. The bishop would never let me.

(LEWIS *stares at him as if he understands, but when he speaks it is clear that nothing* HARRINGTON *has said has gone in)*

LEWIS: I'm going to marry her Harry. If you won't do it, I'll find someone who will.

HARRINGTON: I don't make the rules.

RILEY: Jack. I can't pretend to understand what's happening to you, but if this is what you want, I wish you both happy.

HARRINGTON: I'm really sorry, Jack.

LEWIS: That's alright, Harry. I understand.

(He goes towards the hospital room. RILEY *and* HARRINGTON *exit as the screen rises.* LEWIS *goes back to* JOY's *bedside. The* DOCTOR *has left by now)*

LEWIS: It's me again.

JOY: Did you go?

LEWIS: I went. And I came back.

JOY: This dope they give me. I get confused.

LEWIS: Does it help the pain?

JOY: Oh yes. It's the strangest sensation. Like the pain's still going on down there, but it's nothing to do with me.

LEWIS: Is your mind clear now?

JOY: How would I know? Try me.

LEWIS: What's fifty–eight take away forty–one?

JOY (*wrestling with the sum*): Seventeen?

LEWIS: That's how old I was when you were born.

JOY: I was a baby. You were almost a man. For a while back there, I thought I might just catch you up. But here I am, back to being a baby again.

(*This long speech wears her out and she closes her eyes.* LEWIS *looks lovingly down at her*)

LEWIS: Joy?

JOY: Still here.

LEWIS: I'm going to marry you, Joy. I'm going to marry you before God and the world.

JOY: You don't have to, Jack.

LEWIS: I want to. It's what I want.

JOY: Make an honest woman of me.

LEWIS: Not you, Joy. I'm the one who hasn't been honest. Look what it takes to make me see sense.

JOY: Think I overdid it?

LEWIS: Don't leave me, Joy.

(She smiles. The morphine makes her sleepy. For a moment, she closes her eyes)

JOY: Back home, we have a quaint old custom. When the guy has made up his mind he wants to marry the girl, he asks her. It's called proposing.

LEWIS: It's the same here.

JOY: Did I miss it?

LEWIS *(taking her hand and kissing it):* Will you marry this foolish, frightened, old man, who needs you more than he can bear to say and loves you even though he hardly knows how?

JOY: Okay. Just this once.

(DOUGLAS enters. He stands in silence, watching. WARNIE enters, accompanied by a young PRIEST, who carries a service book. The PRIEST goes to the bedside and opens his book. LEWIS holds JOY's hand. JOY is fully awake now and, though weak, radiantly happy. She speaks the marriage vow clearly and steadily)

JOY: I, Joy, take thee, Jack.

PRIEST: "To have and to hold, from this day forward."

(Behind them, the lights come up in the Other World space and the wardrobe door swings open of

its own accord. Only DOUGLAS *sees this. He turns and stares)*

JOY: To have and to hold, from this day forward.

PRIEST: "For better, for worse."

JOY: For better, for worse.

(DOUGLAS *moves softly away from the group towards the Other World space, as the familiar ritual continues)*

PRIEST: "For richer, for poorer."

JOY: For richer, for poorer.

PRIEST: "In sickness and in health."

JOY: In sickness and in health.

PRIEST: "To love, cherish, and obey."

JOY: To love, cherish, and obey.

PRIEST: "Till death us do part."

JOY: Till death us do part.

(DOUGLAS *has now entered the Other World space, holds up his hand to a tree that grows there and picks from it a glowing magic apple.* WARNIE *steps forward and gives* LEWIS *a ring.* LEWIS *puts the ring on* JOY's *finger)*

PRIEST: "With this ring I thee wed."

LEWIS: With this ring I thee wed.

PRIEST: "With my body I thee worship."

LEWIS: With my body I thee worship.

PRIEST: "With all my worldly goods I thee endow."

LEWIS: With all my worldly goods I thee endow.

(DOUGLAS *carries the magic apple back into the hospital room and kneels at the foot of* JOY's *bed*)

PRIEST: "In the name of the Father . . ."

LEWIS: In the name of the Father . . .

PRIEST: "and of the Son . . ."

LEWIS: and of the Son . . .

PRIEST: "and of the Holy Ghost."

LEWIS: and of the Holy Ghost.

PRIEST: Amen.

LEWIS: Amen.

PRIEST: Those whom God hath joined together, let no man put asunder. For as much as Jack and Joy have consented together in Holy Wedlock and

have made witness of the same before God and this
company, I pronounce that they be Man and Wife
together. In the name of the Father and of the Son
and of the Holy Ghost. Amen.

(JOY *is now asleep again.* WARNIE *and the* PRIEST
exit. LEWIS *kisses* JOY's *forehead and exits. As he
exits,* DOUGLAS *places the magic apple in his mother's hands. Then he bends over her and kisses her.
The light fades on the Other World as the screen
falls and* DOUGLAS *exits. The* DOCTOR *enters and
goes to* LEWIS. *Time has passed)*

DOCTOR: Well, Mr. Lewis, I think I'm in no danger of
overstating the case if I say, no news is good news.
Given the seriousness of her condition, we have
reason to be cautiously optimistic.

LEWIS: I'm sorry, Doctor, but I don't understand a
word you're saying. It would help me if you would
use words I'm familiar with, like "getting better,"
"getting worse." "Dying."

DOCTOR: I'm afraid none of those words meet the
case. What seems to be happening is that the rate
of spread of the disease is slowing down.

LEWIS: You mean she's getting better?

DOCTOR: She's not worse.

LEWIS: Is not–being–worse better than being–
worse?

DOCTOR: Put like that, yes.

LEWIS: Then she's getting better, isn't she?

DOCTOR: Mr. Lewis. You're looking at a train, standing in a station. It may not be moving right now, but trains move. That's how trains are.

LEWIS: What would be a good sign? People do recover from cancer. It has been known.

DOCTOR: Any sign of returning strength. Any sign that the body is rebuilding the diseased bone.

LEWIS: Did you expect her to make it this far?

DOCTOR: You didn't expect her to make it this far, did you?

(LEWIS *accepts this as the* DOCTOR's *attempt at encouragement*)

LEWIS: Thank you, Doctor.

(The DOCTOR *exits.* LEWIS *reenters the hospital room, where* JOY *is now sitting up in bed. He pulls a chair to her bedside and sits down by her.* JOY *is still weak, but in very good spirits)*

LEWIS: I should have brought you something, shouldn't I? Flowers. Grapes. Why grapes, I wonder?

NURSE: Only 5 minutes, Mr. Lewis.

JOY: Just bring me books, Jack. I'm going crazy here. The nurse has been telling me all about her love life. She's been dating this guy for two years. Will he marry her? How far should she let him go without them being at least engaged? I'm telling you, I was sick with excitement. But she doesn't see him again till Saturday, so I need books.

(LEWIS *smiles at her ready chatter. Just looking at her makes him feel happy*)

LEWIS: It strikes me you're rather better.

JOY: Shh! We have to pretend we haven't noticed, or He'll take it away.

LEWIS: So what advice did you give the nurse?

JOY: I said, give him enough to make him want the rest, then nothing till he pays up.

LEWIS: Poor fellow. He hasn't a chance.

JOY *(holding up her hand, to look at her wedding ring):* Jack. If I get better, do I have to give the ring back?

LEWIS: No, that's yours for ever, Joy. For all eternity.

JOY: You don't have to feel sorry for me now.

LEWIS: Not for myself. I just want some time with you, Joy.

JOY: Shh! *(She glances upwards at God, who mustn't hear)* Speaking of Him, how did you square it?

LEWIS: Marrying you?

JOY: Yes. You're not the sort to say, it's wrong, but I want it anyway.

LEWIS: I did think about it, yes. The argument I gave myself went like this. I want to marry Joy, but if she's married to someone else, I can't. Whatever a divorce court decrees, marriage is indissoluble in the eyes of God. But you see, your husband had been married before. If marriage is indissoluble, he's still married to his first wife. If he's still married to his first wife, he can't have married you. Not in the eyes of God. He wasn't free. So you were never really married to him in the first place. (JOY *laughs)* Am I being too clever?

JOY: I think you have one of the great minds of the century.

LEWIS: Well, I know that.

(A NURSE *enters, with screens to put round the bed)*

NURSE: I said five minutes, Mr. Lewis.

(LEWIS *kisses* JOY *and turns to leave, saying to the* NURSE *as he goes)*

LEWIS: Good luck on Saturday.

(LEWIS *exits, as the screen falls.* WARNIE *and* HAR-
RINGTON *enter)*

HARRINGTON: Frankly, I'm worried about him. His
behavior is entirely out of character.

WARNIE: It's been a very great shock to him.

HARRINGTON: That's my point. I know they've become good friends—

WARNIE: Husband and wife.

HARRINGTON: Well, quite. I mean, what can one say?
The woman is dying.

WARNIE: Not anymore.

HARRINGTON: Not dying?

WARNIE: Jack says she's recovering. The cancer has
stopped spreading.

HARRINGTON *(disconcerted by this information):*
That's very good news. Excellent news. So what
will you do, Warnie?

WARNIE: What do you mean?

HARRINGTON: Well, if she makes a full recovery.
Where will you live?

WARNIE: I don't know.

*(This point had not occurred to him. It does now.
RILEY enters. HARRINGTON turns to him, expecting
to find an ally)*

HARRINGTON: Christopher. Excellent news. Mrs.
Gresham is not to die after all.

RILEY: That is good news.

*(He says no more than this, but it is clear he feels
deeply relieved)*

WARNIE: I think we must call her Mrs. Lewis, you
know.

HARRINGTON: If she does recover, we shall chalk it
up as a victory for the power of prayer.

RILEY: I've never quite understood about prayer.
Does God intervene in the world only when
asked?

HARRINGTON: It has been known.

RILEY: And what are the qualifications for divine
aid? Merit? Intense suffering? Persistent prayer? I
mean, how does he choose?

HARRINGTON: I hardly think this is the time or the
place for a theological argument.

RILEY: And if God knows what's best for us anyway,
why do we need to ask? Doesn't He know already?

(LEWIS *enters*)

LEWIS: Doesn't who know what?

HARRINGTON: Jack, thank goodness. Christopher's being Christopherish about prayer.

LEWIS: Prayer? I pray all the time these days. If I stopped praying, I think I'd stop living.

HARRINGTON: And God hears your prayer, doesn't He? We hear Joy's getting better.

LEWIS: Yes. She is.

HARRINGTON: I'm very glad, Jack.

LEWIS: That's not why I pray, Harry. I pray because I can't help myself. I pray because I'm helpless. I pray because the need flows out of me all the time, waking and sleeping. It doesn't change God. It changes me.

RILEY: Now, that I can understand. That's the first sensible thing I've heard anyone say on the subject.

LEWIS: She's getting better, you see. It's quite something. We mustn't expect too much, of course. Mustn't get our hopes up. Shall we go, Warnie?

WARNIE: Ready when you are, Jack.

(HARRINGTON *and* RILEY *exit. The screen rises to reveal the hospital room again.* JOY*'s bed is behind* *the hospital screens.* LEWIS *and* WARNIE *cross to the corridor outside the hospital room. The* DOCTOR *enters.* LEWIS *turns to him eagerly)*

LEWIS: Well, Doctor?

DOCTOR: I think you should come and see for yourself.

LEWIS: See what?

DOCTOR: She's doing rather well, all things considered.

(LEWIS *follows the* DOCTOR *to the screened bed.* WARNIE *stays back, not wanting to intrude.* LEWIS *stands before the closed screens, as the* DOCTOR *draws them back. The bed is empty.* JOY *stands beside the bed, supported by crutches, and attended by the watchful* NURSE)

LEWIS: Rather well!

JOY: Hello, Jack. Warnie.

LEWIS: Look at you. Come on now. Show us. *(She walks a few cautious steps.* WARNIE, *the* DOCTOR *and the* NURSE *clap.* LEWIS *turns to them like a proud parent.)* Did you see that, Warnie? Did you?

WARNIE: Good show, Joy. Good show.

LEWIS: Do some more.

DOCTOR: Slowly now.

LEWIS: Of course, of course. That's enough. Rest.

(The NURSE *helps* JOY *to the side of the bed.* LEWIS *goes to the* DOCTOR)

LEWIS: When can I take her home?

DOCTOR: As soon as you like. I see no reason to keep her in hospital, so long as the remission continues.

LEWIS: Which is how long?

(The DOCTOR *glances towards* JOY)

LEWIS: You can speak openly. She does have an interest in the matter.

DOCTOR: It could be weeks. It could be months.

LEWIS: Why not years?

DOCTOR: In such an advanced case, that would be . . . unusual. I'm sorry. You did want to know.

LEWIS: Right. We take what we can get. *(He goes to* JOY) How would you like to come home?

JOY: Where's home, Jack?

LEWIS: My house. Our house. You're my wife, remember? Warnie and I are going to look after you.

JOY: Have you asked Warnie?

LEWIS: Ah. *(He goes over to* WARNIE*)* Ah, Warnie
. . . there's something I'd like to put to you . . .

WARNIE: Don't worry about me, Jack. I'll sort myself
out.

LEWIS: Sort yourself out? What do you mean?

WARNIE: New digs. No problem.

LEWIS: Do you want to?

WARNIE: As you wish, Jack.

LEWIS: I don't.

WARNIE: Right you are.

LEWIS: That's settled, then.

(WARNIE *kisses* JOY)

WARNIE: See you at home, Joy.

(He exits)

(JOY *stands.* LEWIS *takes her suitcase. They walk
downstage with the* NURSE *as the screen comes
down behind them)*

JOY: Thank you for everything, Mrs. Braddock.

LEWIS: Yes. Thank you for everything.

JOY: Not bad?

LEWIS: Not bad. Now I don't want to hear any talk of miracles.

JOY: Why not? It's a miracle to me.

LEWIS: Miracles frighten me.

JOY: Take it when it's offered, I say.

LEWIS: I'm frightened of loving God too much for giving you back to me. That way, I could just as easily hate God, later.

JOY: Don't be so hard on yourself, Jack. Thank God now, and let later come later.

LEWIS: Anyway, it's not such a big miracle, really. You coming back to life.

JOY: What's wrong with it? You leave my miracle alone.

LEWIS: You were alive before. I wasn't.

JOY: What are you talking about?

LEWIS: I started living when I started loving you, Joy. That makes me only a few months old.

JOY: Could be a short life, Jack.

LEWIS: At least it's a life. *(The screen rises to reveal the study at the Kilns. They enter)* Welcome home!

JOY: It really does feel like home.

LEWIS: Oh does it? I am pleased.

JOY: Jack. I have a question I've never dared ask before. But now that we're married . . .

LEWIS: Anything, Joy.

JOY: Do you ever turn the heat on in here?

LEWIS: I'm afraid it's broken.

JOY: When did it stop working?

LEWIS: Good heavens, I can't remember. Ten years ago? Put your coat on, I always do.

JOY: This world is not a perfect place, Jack. And your house is less perfect than most of it. Will you let me purge it a little?

LEWIS: It's your home now, Joy. Purge away.

(She hits chair with cane. Dust rises)

JOY: Look at that. *(She turns to him and strokes his shoulder)* And how about you? I'm not caressing you lovingly, I'm removing the dust. Actually, I am caressing you lovingly. *(They look into each other's eyes. They embrace and kiss.* LEWIS *then helps her into her chair, brings a footstool for her legs and covers her with an afghan. He then brings her a crossword puzzle and a pen)* Such service. I should get sick more often.

(LEWIS *exits, carrying one of her canes away.* WARNIE *enters, reading a newspaper and settles down in his usual chair.* DOUGLAS *enters, carrying a chess board, set up with chess pieces, which he sets beside* WARNIE's *chair. He ponders the game.* WARNIE *reads aloud from his newspaper)*

WARNIE: "The Queen has announced that the Royal Family's surname will be changed to Mountbatten–Windsor."

JOY: Quintessence. Botanically expressed. Four.

WARNIE: Used to be something foreign. Then it became Windsor. Pith.

JOY: Pith.

WARNIE: "The new surname will not apply until Prince Charles has grandsons." How very strange.

(WARNIE *makes a move in the chess game.* LEWIS *has reentered and stands behind* DOUGLAS, *watching the game)*

DOUGLAS: Oh no! I didn't see that! Can't I have my move again?

LEWIS: You don't need to. Look. Check.

DOUGLAS: Oh yes.

JOY: Jack, make him work it out for himself. It's the only way he'll learn.

LEWIS: Is that so, Joy? Maybe we should send him to the University of Hard Knocks. He could learn to say, "I don't know much about art, but I call a spade a spade."

JOY: I knew it! That Honest Jack act you pull on your radio talks, it's all a front. You're an intellectual snob.

LEWIS: Oh really? And am I a "highbrow," and a "smug academic"?

JOY: I'm not insulting you Jack. I'm criticizing you.

LEWIS: I see. Please enlighten me.

JOY: The educational system in this country is prehistoric. The boys at Douglas's school talk about going to a university like it was going to the moon.

LEWIS: How is that a criticism of me? I'd like as many boys to go to university as possible.

JOY: I count three buried assumptions there. "I'd like"—that's the language of mild preference, not active concern. You don't say, "I'd like as many boys to be saved from starvation as possible."

LEWIS: My language reflects—

JOY: Wait. I haven't finished. Second buried assumption: "boys." What about girls?

LEWIS: Conceded. Go on.

JOY: Third buried assumption: you'd like as many to go to university "as possible." What makes it possible, Jack? God? Chance? The weather? How about people like you? The high priests of the sacred cult of the intellectual elite.

LEWIS: Verbal raspberries.

JOY: Dismissive images. You always want the last word.

LEWIS: Precious hope of that.

WARNIE: Honeymoon.

JOY: What?

LEWIS: What was that, Warnie?

WARNIE: Marriage. Honeymoon. That's the way of it. You should have a honeymoon.

LEWIS: Joy's not up to traveling.

JOY: I suppose this is our honeymoon, Warnie.

LEWIS: I suppose it is.

JOY: So how come we're carrying on as if we've been married for years?

LEWIS: Is that what we're doing?

JOY: You are an intellectual bully, you know.

LEWIS: That makes two of us. I think I'm too old to change now. Do you mind?

JOY: You being too old or you being a bully?

LEWIS: Either.

JOY: No. I don't mind. Do you mind?

LEWIS: No. I don't want to be young any more. When you're young, you're always looking ahead, always waiting for something better to come round the next bend in the road. I'm not looking ahead any more. I'm with you, here, now, and that's enough.

JOY: People go on journeys for their honeymoon, Jack.

LEWIS: What, you mean abroad?

JOY: No need to sound so alarmed.

LEWIS: My mother took Warnie and me to Berneval, near Dieppe, the summer before she died. My one and only holiday abroad.

WARNIE: Nineteen hundred and seven.

JACK: Where do you want to go?

JOY: I've always wanted to go to Greece. To see the Parthenon. And the Temple of Apollo at Delphi. And the lion gates of Mycenae.

LEWIS: Where would we stay?

JOY: Some little Greek hotel.

LEWIS: Are you up to it?

JOY: Me? If you are.

LEWIS: I truly believe that if I had to go into a hotel with a woman and sign the register, I'd blush.

WARNIE: That's settled, then.

JOY: The isles of Greece. The isles of Greece.

(As JOY *and* LEWIS *move downstage, the screen falls behind them)*

JOY AND LEWIS: Where burning Sappho loved and
   sung
   Where grew the arts of war and peace
   Where Delos rose and Phoebus sprung
   Eternal summer gilds them yet
   But all except their sun is set.

JOY: And there it is as advertised, not yet set. I love the sun. Don't you love the sun?

LEWIS: Dreadful glare, isn't there?

(A WAITER has entered with their luggage)

LEWIS: I never feel at ease in hotels. There's always someone hanging around trying to be helpful.

JOY: Well, I like them. And I especially like room service.

LEWIS: Room service? I always used to believe that room service was saying prayers in bed.

JOY: Well, you order some prayers if you want. Me, I want a gin and tonic.

LEWIS: Now? You only just had breakfast.

JOY: So?

LEWIS *(to WAITER)*: Alright. I'd like to order some drinks, if we may, to be brought up to our room, if that's convenient. We'd like a gin and tonic, and a gin and tonic. So that's two gin and tonics . . . actually, two gins and tonic, that is, to be strictly accurate, and I think one should strive to be, don't you?

(The WAITER leaves)

JOY: You don't drink gin.

LEWIS: Yes, I know. I'm afraid I panicked.

JOY: I love the sun. People used to worship the sun. I can understand it.

LEWIS: Well, I can understand people who worship the sun in England where the sun is invisible, but here. Look at it, hanging around like a waiter hoping for a tip. This has no class. No mystery.

JOY: No, Jack. It's a feeling. You just don't know how to be in the sun.

LEWIS: What do you mean?

JOY: Come here and I'll show you.

LEWIS: You know I don't like surprises.

JOY: Come over here.

LEWIS: This isn't going to work.

JOY: Now put that face of yours up here. Feel it on your face. The sun so close you could stick out your tongue and lick it. No words. No thoughts. Just the sun on your face. The sound of the wind in the olive trees, and the cicadas.

LEWIS: Cicadas.

JOY: Potatoes. Potahtoes. In this land, nothing is impossible. Nothing is forbidden. You could even take off your coat.

LEWIS: Oh, I say, steady on.

JOY: Take it off. Take it off. All off.

(The WAITER *enters with drinks, as* JOY *tries to remove* LEWIS's *jacket)*

LEWIS: Joy, not now. I'm perfectly alright. Look out, there's somebody there. *(To* WAITER) Sorry about that. (LEWIS *hands* JOY *a drink)* You all right?

JOY: I'm fine. I'm great.

(LEWIS *hands drinks back to the* WAITER. *As the screen rises,* LEWIS *and* JOY *turn and head into the garden at home)*

JOY: I am so happy. I don't think I've ever been so happy in my life.

LEWIS: Nor I. Not since the day I was elected a Fellow of Magdalen.

JOY: No kidding! I didn't think there was any experience to beat that this side of paradise.

LEWIS: This is paradise for me. Now.

JOY: Don't say that, Jack. Paradise lasts, I hope. It's beautiful here. Being with you is everything I want. But it's not going to last.

LEWIS: We don't need to think of that now. I don't want to spoil the time we have together.

JOY: It doesn't spoil it. It makes it precious. The small things. The ordinary things. Each time you touch me, I feel it like a shock. Your nearness. Your reality. You. *(She looks at him, forcing him to face what is coming)* What will you do when I die?

LEWIS: I don't know.

JOY: I want to be with you then, Jack. The only way I can do that is to talk to you about it now.

LEWIS: I shall manage. Don't worry about me.

JOY: I think it can be better than that. Better than just managing. What I'm trying to say is that pain, then, is part of this happiness, now. That's the deal.

LEWIS: We'll have no clocks. No calendars. No clocks.

JOY: I know your footsteps. I can tell it's you, long before you reach the house. I know it's you coming up the road.

LEWIS: I never thought I could be so happy, so late in life. Every day when I come home, there you are.

JOY: The first words you speak, I know what kind of a mood you're in. Just from the sound of your voice. I watch you when you're working at your desk. I study you. I learn you.

LEWIS: Everyday. Everyday when I come home, there you are. I can't get used to that. Every day it surprises me. There you are. It's the sheer avail-

ability of the happiness that takes my breath away.
I reach out and there you are. I hold you in my
arms. I kiss you. All I have to do is reach out and
there you are. You've made the world kind to me
and I'm so grateful. Grateful for all the ordinary
domestic pleasures. *(The pain returns to* JOY. *She
feels it, but tries not to show it)* I think I love you
too much, Joy. I can't bear to see you in pain.

JOY: The pain doesn't matter. It keeps me quiet.

LEWIS: When it gets close, you find out whether you
believe or not.

JOY: Only shadows, Jack. That's what you're always
saying. Real life hasn't begun yet. You'd just better
be right.

(She slips into an exhausted sleep. DOUGLAS *enters)*

LEWIS: Oh, Douglas. Your mother's very sick, I'm
afraid.

DOUGLAS: She's going to die, isn't she? (LEWIS
doesn't know how to respond) Why?

LEWIS: I don't know.

DOUGLAS: Can't you do something?

LEWIS: I'm afraid not.

DOUGLAS: Okay.

(He exits. LEWIS *draws a chair up beside* JOY *and sits down. For a few moments, he watches her. Then he drifts into a half sleep, exhausted himself. The lighting changes slowly, to nighttime.* JOY *opens her eyes. She is very weak)*

JOY: Still here?

LEWIS *(waking):* Still here.

JOY: Go to bed. Get some sleep.

LEWIS: Soon.

JOY: Jack. Has it been worth it?

LEWIS: Three years of happiness?

JOY: Tell me you'll be alright.

LEWIS: I'll be alright.

JOY: Can we talk about it?

LEWIS: We've never pretended with each other.

JOY: No. Never pretended.

LEWIS: Are you afraid?

JOY: Of dying?

LEWIS: Yes.

JOY: I'm tired, Jack. I want to rest. I just don't want to leave you.

LEWIS: I don't want you to go.

JOY: Too much pain.

LEWIS: I know.

JOY: Other worlds. It has to be more than we can imagine. Even more than you can imagine.

LEWIS: Far more.

JOY: I love your other worlds, Jack. That was how I first fell in love with you. Long before I met you.

LEWIS: Just stories, Joy.

JOY: Magical stories.

LEWIS: I don't know what to do, Joy. You'll have to tell me what to do.

JOY: You have to let me go, Jack.

LEWIS: I'm not sure that I can.

(A silence. JOY *is in too much pain to speak. Then the thought of her son breaks through, bringing another sort of pain)*

JOY: Douglas—will you take care of—

LEWIS: Of course I will, Joy.

JOY: He pretends not to mind.

LEWIS: I know.

JOY: Like you.

LEWIS: No pretending anymore.

JOY: I've loved you so much, Jack. (LEWIS *takes her hand and presses it to his lips, trying not to show his own pain)* It's always easier for the one who goes first.

(He can see that the effort of talking is too much for her)

LEWIS: Don't talk any more. You rest.

(She nods her head and closes her eyes. By now all we can see are the two of them, deep in the night. LEWIS sits with his chin resting in his hands, speaking softly into the darkness)

LEWIS: Not much more to say. I love you, Joy. I love you so much. You've made me so happy. I didn't know I could be so happy. You're the truest person I've ever known. Sweet Jesus, be with my beloved wife, Joy. Forgive me if I love her too much. Have mercy on us both.

(JOY's eyes open. She speaks very faintly)

JOY: Get some sleep, Jack.

LEWIS: How's the pain?

JOY: Not too good. Only shadows.

LEWIS: Only shadows.

(Her eyes close again. LEWIS *rises, stoops and kisses her, and walks softly out of the pool of light. The light on* JOY *fades slowly to black, as the screen comes in)*

HARRINGTON: Naturally I wouldn't say this to Jack, but better sooner than later. Better quick than slow. After all, there was no question about it. The writing was on the wall.

GREGG: Is he taking it very hard?

HARRINGTON: He's a remarkable man, Jack. Faith solid as a rock.

RILEY: Harry, those few well–chosen words at the church. Did I hear you correctly? It seemed to me that you said something like "All who knew her loved her."

HARRINGTON: Something like that.

RILEY: Not quite God's own truth, was it?

HARRINGTON: Good grief, Christopher, what was I supposed to say? That nobody could stand her?

RILEY: Jack loved her. That's what's true and that's what matters. But I didn't and you didn't.

HARRINGTON: She is dead.

RILEY: Death does not improve the character.

(The screen goes up and they join WARNIE *and* GREGG *who are seated at the college high table)*

GREGG: You don't love anyone, Christopher, as far as I can see.

RILEY: That may well be true, but Harry still shouldn't tell whoppers.

HARRINGTON: Jack was standing six feet away.

RILEY: Jack wouldn't have minded. He's changed. She did that. She was a remarkable woman. But I'm damned if I'm going to start liking her just because she's dead.

HARRINGTON: Did you like her, Warnie?

WARNIE: Not at first. But oh, yes.

*(*LEWIS *enters. An awkward silence falls as he comes to his place at table)*

LEWIS: I wasn't going to come. Then I thought I would.

(He sits. He sounds perfectly calm)

HARRINGTON: Life must go on.

LEWIS: I don't know that it must. But it certainly does.

GREGG: I'm sorry I wasn't able to be at the church.

LEWIS: Not important, Alan.

HARRINGTON: My little address, Jack. Was it . . . ?

LEWIS: Please forgive me, Harry. I haven't the slightest idea what you said in church. I didn't hear a word.

HARRINGTON: Fine. Fine. Perfectly understandable.

RILEY: Are you alright, Jack?

LEWIS: No.

HARRINGTON: Thank God for your faith, Jack. Where would you be without that?

LEWIS: I'd be here, drinking my port.

HARRINGTON: What I mean to say, Jack, is that it's only faith that makes any sense of times like this.

LEWIS (putting down his glass): No, I'm sorry, Harry, but that won't do. This is a mess, and that's all there is to it.

HARRINGTON: A mess?

LEWIS: What sense do you make of it? You tell me.

HARRINGTON: But, Jack—we have to have faith that God knows—

LEWIS: God knows. Yes, God knows. I don't doubt that. God knows. But does God care? Did he care about Joy?

HARRINGTON: Why are you talking like this, Jack? We can't see what's best for us. You know that. We're not the Creator.

LEWIS: No. We're the creatures. We're the rats in the cosmic laboratory. I've no doubt the great experiment is for our own good, eventually, but that still makes God the vivisectionist.

HARRINGTON: This is your grief talking.

LEWIS: What was talking before? My complacency?

HARRINGTON: Please, Jack. Please.

LEWIS: I'm sorry, Harry. You're a good man. I don't mean to distress you. But the fact is, I've come up against a bit of experience recently. Experience is a brutal teacher, but you learn fast. I'm sorry. I shouldn't have come this evening. I'm not fit company. *(He rises)* If you'll forgive me.

(He leaves the table)

WARNIE: Excuse me.

(WARNIE *follows his brother to where he stands, frowning, by himself. The screen falls*)

LEWIS: Sorry about that, Warnie. Not necessary.

WARNIE: Everybody understands, Jack.

LEWIS: I can't see her any more. I can't remember her face. What's happening to me?

WARNIE: I expect it's shock.

LEWIS: I'm so terribly afraid. Of never seeing her again. Of thinking that suffering is just suffering after all. No cause. No purpose. No pattern. No sense. Just pain, in a world of pain.

WARNIE: I don't know what to tell you, Jack.

LEWIS: Nothing. There's nothing to say.

(*They are silent for a few moments.* DOUGLAS *enters on the far side of the stage. He is profoundly hurt by his mother's death, but is refusing to show it*)

WARNIE: Jack.

LEWIS: Yes.

WARNIE: About Douglas.

LEWIS: Yes.

WARNIE: Your grief is your business. Maybe you feel life is a mess. Maybe it is. But he's only a child.

LEWIS: What am I supposed to do about it?

WARNIE: Talk to him.

LEWIS: I don't know what to say to him.

WARNIE: Just talk to him.

(WARNIE *exits.* LEWIS *walks slowly across to* DOUGLAS. *He speaks to the boy in a matter-of-fact way, as if they are equals*)

LEWIS: When I was your age, my mother died. That was cancer, too. I thought that if I prayed for her to get better, and if I really believed she'd get better, then she wouldn't die. But she did.

DOUGLAS: It doesn't work.

LEWIS: No. It doesn't work.

DOUGLAS: I don't care.

LEWIS: I do. When I'm alone, I start crying. Do you cry?

DOUGLAS: No.

LEWIS: I didn't when I was your age. *(A brief pause)* I loved your mother very much.

DOUGLAS: That's okay.

LEWIS: I loved her too much. She knew that. She said to me, 'Is it worth it?' She knew how it would be later. It doesn't seem fair, does it? If you want the love, you have to have the pain.

DOUGLAS: I don't see why she had to get sick.

LEWIS: Nor I. You can't hold onto things. You have to let them go.

DOUGLAS: Jack?

LEWIS: Yes.

DOUGLAS: Do you believe in heaven?

LEWIS: Yes.

DOUGLAS: I don't believe in heaven.

LEWIS: That's okay.

DOUGLAS: I sure would like to see her again.

LEWIS: Me too.

(DOUGLAS *can't take any more. He reaches out for comfort, pressing himself against* LEWIS. LEWIS *wraps his arms around the boy and at last his own tears break through, in heartbreaking sobs, unloosing the grief of a lifetime. His emotion releases the tears that have been waiting in the boy. As they fall quiet,* DOUGLAS *detaches himself and exits.* LEWIS *turns to face the audience and begins to speak quietly. His words are a version of the talk he has given earlier, now transformed by his own suffering)*

LEWIS: We are like blocks of stone, out of which the sculptor carves the forms of men. The blows of his chisel, which hurt us so much, are what makes us perfect.

No shadows here. Only darkness, and silence, and the pain that cries like a child.

It ends, like all affairs of the heart, with exhaustion. Only so much pain is possible. Then, rest.

So it comes about that, when I am quiet, when I am quiet, she returns to me. There she is, in my mind, in my memory, coming towards me and I love her again as I did before, even though I know I will lose her again, and be hurt again.

So you can say if you like that Jack Lewis has no answer to the question after all, except this: I have been given the choice twice in my life. The boy chose safety. The man chooses suffering.

(He now speaks to her, in his memory)

I went to my wardrobe this morning. I was looking for my old brown jacket, the one I used to wear before—I'd forgotten that you'd carried out one of

your purges there. Just before we went to Greece,
I think it was.

I find I can live with the pain, after all. The pain,
now, is part of the happiness, then. That's the deal.

Only shadows, Joy.

Final curtain.